FOULSHAM'S HOME LIBRARY

SPEECHES & TOASTS FOR ALL OCCASIONS

HOW TO PREPARE AND HOW TO DELIVER THEM WITH NUMEROUS EXAMPLES

A PRACTICAL AND UP-TO-DATE GUIDE TO PUBLIC SPEAKING

LONDON
W. FOULSHAM & CO. LTD.

MADE IN GREAT BRITAIN
BY PURNELL AND SONS, LTD., PAULTON (SOMERSET) AND LONDON

PREFACE

HOW TO USE THIS BOOK

WE will suppose that you are shortly to attend a function and have been asked to make a speech or propose a certain toast ; maybe, you are required to reply to a toast. Whichever is the case, this book will help you if you use it as follow :

First : Look down the index and see if a specimen of the exact speech, toast, or reply is given. If so, your discourse is already prepared for you, and there is no reason why you should not deliver it exactly as it stands. Personally, we advise you to paraphrase it closely, and, as a rule, it is best to embody a few personal details. In other words, make it slightly longer than it is given in this book, but adhere to the opening and closing passages. Be careful not to commence with "Ladies and Gentlemen" if, say, there are no ladies present.

Next, read the chapter on "Delivering a Speech," and, if you are in any doubt on such matters, read also the part dealing with "Pronunciation."

Second : If your subject does not figure among the specimens, there must be one that will come very close to it, for the specimens have been carefully chosen to cover a wide field. Take the one that is most allied to yours and adapt it to your subject. Be guided by the paragraph of hints and run your eye down the list of "Useful Quotations" to see if there be any that apply in your case. A few apt quotations in a speech give it body.

Third : You may prefer to use none of the set specimens, but to compose your own speech entirely. In this case read the chapter on "Preparing a Speech," and then proceed according to the instructions. Even in this case the specimens will help you, and it will be wise to note their construction.

There are many useful quotations scattered throughout the book. It may be well to point out that in certain cases a speaker should only use them to contradict them. We do not pretend to agree with their reasoning in every instance.

Fourth: You may be called upon to take the chair at a meeting or act as secretary. These are very onerous positions to hold if you are not acquainted with the routine of the duties. There are two detailed chapters dealing with this work, and once you have studied them all difficulties should disappear.

CONTENTS

CHAPTER I

CHAPTER II

CHAPTER III

CHAPTER IV

CHAPTER V

CHAPTER VI

CHAPTER VII

CHAPTER VIII

CHAPTER IX

CHAPTER X

CHAPTER XI

CHAPTER XII

SPEECHES & TOASTS

CHAPTER I

PREPARING A SPEECH

IN your preliminary attempts at speech-making you may find that notes are more hindering than helpful. In overcoming your nervousness, short narratives and descriptions—spoken essays, in fact—will serve as the best exercises. From these you may progress to short criticisms of, or replies to, other persons' speeches. But at this stage the necessity for brief notes will make itself apparent; and as soon as you feel confident enough to discuss a subject at some length, this preparation of the necessary notes must engage your attention.

In roughing out a speech there are several rules to be remembered. The point to be established must always be borne in mind, and every argument used should bear directly upon, and lead rationally up to, that point.

Digression of any kind must be rigidly excluded. Excursions into bypaths tend to distract the minds of your hearers, and possibly your own mind, from the main theme. They also use up time unprofitably. Every fresh fact or argument should proceed easily and logically from that preceding it; and it is in enabling you to ensure this that notes are of greatest value.

It has been said that the best advice on making a speech is embodied in the injunction to "stand up, speak up, and shut up." And very truly, too, for there is a great deal more in the phrase than is at once apparent. To stand up physically you will have already learnt. But you have still to stand up to your subject, to deal with it fairly, squarely, and thoroughly. Speaking up, also, applies as much to the substance of your discourse as to the manner of its delivery; you must ensure that your method of treatment is worthy of the subject you expound and the audience you address. And to shut up is not the easiest part of a speaker's task. Simply to dry up because your supply of ideas has run out will undo any good you may have achieved. Your various arguments have to be brought together and rounded off in a climax, which will leave your hearers with a clear-cut impression of unassailable logic arriving at an absolutely right conclusion. Having reached your culminating point, you should never on any pretext return to go over old ground.

The arrangement of your notes should conduce to all these desired excellences. A few ideas jotted down anyhow will be much more likely to confuse than to assist you. Care expended in preparing notes will help you in two ways. The preparation will serve practically as a rehearsal of the speech, fixing the ideas strongly in your brain; the notes themselves, when referred to, will be immediately intelligible and a real help.

Before proceeding, however, with the preparation of notes, a clear understanding of the essential component parts of a speech must be obtained. These parts may be regarded as being six in number, each following rationally from that preceding, all in direct relation to each other and the whole. They are as follow:

(1) General introduction of subject.

(2) Statement of the particular proposition which is to be expounded.

(3) The evidence in detail.

(4) The summary of evidence.

(5) Exposition of the conclusion logically to be drawn from such evidence.

(6) The appeal for support, or the "peroration."

Under these headings your notes may most conveniently be set down. Naturally, certain of the divisions are capable of further subdivision. Evidence in detail, for instance, may well have six divisions of its own, the number being mainly dependent on its bulk.

Let us suppose, for the purpose of a practical example, that you have to deliver a speech on " The Need for Prison Reform." Having acquired a fair knowledge of your subject, you come to the preparation of your notes.

First comes the question of how to open. Your introduction must be of a nature to arrest attention. Some topical or personal reference will generally achieve this end, and is the method very frequently adopted. In the present instance it will do very well.

Now, then, for the first note. Since the question is of prisons, recent police proceedings will supply a topical reference. Select a case that has received a fair amount of press comment, and under the first of the headings mentioned above, write down :

(1) John Smith, burglar. 3 years.

Having mentioned this case in opening your speech, you have to lead up to the subject of Prisons. On prisons few people have very definite ideas. You may bring this home to them by asking whether they have any idea where, and to what, John Smith is going. Very good ; write as a second note, under the same heading :

Where is he going ?

You will be able to enlarge on this somewhat, calling to mind possibly the description of the contemporary prisons contained in Charles Reade's novel " It Is Never Too Late To Mend." Here is a further note to make. Under your heading of General Introduction you have, then, this :

(1) John Smith, burglar. 3 years.
Where is he going ?
" It Is Never Too Late To Mend."

Passing to heading (2) you have to set out your "argument" or the proposition you wish to prove. For this, bearing in mind that you wish to show that our prisons need reform, you had best give some reason why as at present constituted they are wrong. You think, perhaps, that it is because they do not have the requisite effect. Surely they ought to improve criminals, not merely punish them in a spirit of vindictiveness. That offenders are not improved by periods of imprisonment is shown by the continual mention in the Press of persons who have twenty or thirty convictions, and who have spent the greater portion of their lives in jail. Under (2), then, write down:

(2) Prisons need reform.
They do not improve criminals.
Shown by repeated convictions.

With (3) we come to the presentment of the evidence you have acquired by reading up your subject, or in other ways. Its quantity will be governed by your time-limit to a certain extent; but if the time allowed you is short, you should economize it by compressing details rather than by omitting them. Your notes of evidence will appear something like this:

(3) Food in prison is the absolute minimum.
Punishment entails reduction of food (starvation).
Silence is enforced (mental torture).
Solitary confinement (ditto).
Condemned man's 3 weeks of terrible suspense (ditto).
Divine Service is a farce.
Attempts at uplift (ditto).
New offenders are thrown in with the old.

On each of these sub-headings you should be able to discourse for two minutes or more, forcing your hearers to realize what these things mean.

For the summary of this evidence it will merely be necessary to make a note thus:

(4) Physical and mental torture.
No genuine attempt to improve criminals.
Contamination.

The logical conclusion from all the foregoing is that the system does no good (actual harm, rather), is cruel, and is therefore in need of reform. Make a simple note to the effect:

(5) System does harm.
Is cruel.
Vast improvement obviously necessary.

Your peroration should have all the eloquence of which you are capable; and, as a keynote, you might jot down as a final aid:

(6) Ignorance of the facts alone could permit such frightfulness in a really civilized country.

As a whole, your notes will appear thus:

(1) *General Introduction.*
John Smith, burglar. 3 years.
Where is he going?
"It Is Never Too Late To Mend."

(2) *Statement of Particular Proposition to be Expounded.*
Prison system needs reform.
It does not improve criminals.
Shown by repeated convictions.

(3) *The Evidence in Detail.*
Food in prison the absolute minimum.
Punishment entails reduction of food (starvation).
Silence is enforced (mental torture).
Solitary confinement (ditto).
Condemned man's 3 weeks of terrible suspense (ditto).
Divine Service is a farce.
Attempts at uplift (ditto).
New offenders are thrown in with the old.

(4) *Summary of Evidence.*
Physical and mental torture.
No genuine attempt to improve criminals.
Contamination.

(5) *Exposition of Logical Conclusion from Evidence.*
System does harm.
Is cruel.
Vast improvement obviously necessary.

(6) *Peroration.*
Ignorance of facts alone could permit such frightfulness in a really civilized country.

If your memory is good, or if you have had some little experience, the above could advantageously be cut down to:

(1) John Smith. Charles Reade.
(2) Reform. No improving effect. Repeated convictions.
(3) Food. Solitary. Silence. 3 weeks. Moral teachings farce. Contamination.
(4) Torture. Fail to uplift. Make worse.
(5) Harmful. Cruel. REFORM.
(6) Frightfulness—civilization.

A beginner would be ill-advised, however, to attempt a speech from notes cut down to this extent. The longer form is clearer, and if well spaced and arranged can hardly mislead him.

In part (2) of a speech it is usually necessary, besides stating your proposition, to define the terms used therein. In the example used this was not necessary; but had your subject been, say, "Flaws in Tariff Reform," it would have been necessary to explain what you meant by "flaws" and by "tariff reform." Omitting to define your terms will almost invariably ensure your being misunderstood.

The "peroration" is the appeal to the heart made after all possible has been done by appealing to reason. Speakers who do not possess the gift of rhetoric are best advised to close with a quiet request for a verdict on the evidence shown.

Before leaving the subject it must be admitted that some authorities advise that a beginner should write out the whole of his speech, commit it to memory, and have the whole of the manuscript with him for reference when his ordeal arrives. It is true that some of our most brilliant speakers have followed this practice; and it is also true that the most striking phrases of any speech are more often the result of deliberate preparation than of the inspiration of the moment. The practice is, nevertheless, not commended herein, as it so often leads to flat, monotonous delivery, and to complete confusion in the event of the speaker "losing his place."

Chapter II

DELIVERING A SPEECH

MANY people find no difficulty in expressing themselves fluently in conversation, but the moment they rise to make a speech they go to pieces and flounder about in a sea of bewilderment.

As a matter of fact, orators are made more frequently than they are born, so that the budding speech-maker should take heart and attend to a few simple rules. The first thing of all is to have good subject-matter to say. Without it no amount of oratory will be of avail. Under the previous head, we showed how a speech should be prepared, and most of the pages which follow are devoted to specimens which can be delivered either as they stand or altered to suit particular circumstances. There should be no difficulty, then, with the subject-matter.

The next point is " How to Make the Speech." Many of us are nervous at addressing an audience. Personally, I believe that most of the best orators are nervous at first. The question is how to overcome this unpleasant failing. Well, it is useful to tell yourself that you have prepared a rattling good speech with many real " hits " in it. If you impress that on your mind, it will go a long way towards giving you confidence. If you begin to wonder whether what you are going to say is interesting or not you will stand a good chance of going to pieces. So do not allow such questions to enter your mind.

When your speech has been prepared, go into an empty room, far away from everybody, and deliver it as you think it should be delivered. Make your points, one after another, from your notes and reason out aloud the various passages. If you miss a point, go back and put things right. In this way you can work up the speech to a good pitch of perfection. Now persuade a few people—brothers, sisters, your wife, anybody interested in your success, in fact—to listen to a trial run. Ask for their opinions at the end and be guided by such criticism. By this time you will have brushed away many of the awkward passages and the thing will begin to assume the professional touch.

If, just before you are about to rise on the momentous occasion, you feel nervy, deflate the lungs, then take in a full breath of air and expel it slowly. This will put more than the usual supply of oxygen into your blood, and it will have the effect of steadying the nerves. Try it and you will be surprised.

But the man or woman who wants to become a good public speaker should go through a course of training. To read aloud passages from good books is one of the finest exercises that can be attempted by oneself; while the joining of a local debating society is, of course, invaluable.

Although reading aloud is a useful exercise, it should be remembered that a speech ought not to be delivered as though it were read. There should be more halting, more acting in a speech than in reading. "Ladies and gentlemen," you will commence, "I don't know why I have been chosen to propose the health of So-and-So." And in making this remark you ought to look somewhat mystified and appear at a loss to know why you have been selected. You act, in fact. Then, again, you should make use of gestures when a point is to be emphasized. But the gestures must not be noisy ones. The orator who smacks a fist in the palm of his hand and so creates a bang is a "park orator" and should not be copied. The man who hits the dispatch box in the House of Commons—we all know him—is even worse.

Another thing to remember is to change the whole tone of your voice when you reach the end of your conversational matter and turn to the actual words of the toast. You are saying, for instance, ". . . and I am sure you all agree with my remarks. Ladies and gentlemen, I ask you to fill your glasses and drink deeply to the toast of So-and-So." Up to the word "remarks" your pitch is, more than likely, fairly high. After this word you pause for a second and then begin with the word "Ladies" in a lower, more dramatic key.

Of course you must enunciate clearly every word uttered. Some of the most flowery speakers in the House of Commons drop their voices almost to a whisper while saying the last three or four words. Naturally, it is very vexing to have to guess them; often it spoils the whole speech.

Your attitude counts for something. Don't loll; don't plunge your hands in your pockets if you are a man; and don't roll your eyes. A good upright position will help you and give the audience a good impression of you.

You should try to speak without notes of any kind; but if you feel you may break down have them ready. In really desperate cases have the speech written out in full and just read it. Of course, a speech that is read seldom rings true. We remember a case in point. A member of a big city company was asked to speak at a public gathering. He took a roll of papers from his tail pocket, adjusted his glasses, and began to read: "It is with considerable surprise that I see so many faces of old friends before me." The old friends laughed.

In conclusion, remember the advice of Hamlet to his players:

"Speak the speech, I pray you, as I pronounced it to you, trippingly on the tongue; but if you mouth it . . . I had as lief the town-crier spoke my lines. Nor do not saw the air too much with your hand, thus; but use all gently . . . Be not too tame neither, but let your own discretion be your tutor: suit the action to the word, the word to the action: with this special observance, that you o'erstep not the modesty of nature."

Chapter III

PRONUNCIATION, VOCABULARY, AND STYLE

REFINEMENT of speech is necessary to all who would become good public speakers. And here it may be said that the possession of a brogue or accent such as that of an Irishman or Northerner should by no means be considered a defect; for, given that a speaker uses good grammatical construction, and does not actually mispronounce words, his brogue not infrequently lends a distinct charm to his discourse.

The use of the aspirate, however, and the pronunciation of some of the more unfamiliar of our words are matters that require attention from almost every one. It is quite common to hear such expressions as "izzee" for "is he," and "he-oo" for "he who"; these are the very natural results of rapid and slurred speech, and will disappear if a speaker will but remember to deliver each word separately and deliberately. A far more irritating defect, and one much more difficult to eradicate, is the habit of misplacing the aspirate. In their desire not to omit it, some people tack the letter "h" on to almost every word beginning with a vowel. Since it is mainly the outcome of nervousness, this fault is more easy of correction after the speaker has gained some confidence from his initial attempts. He should practise by reading aloud very slowly some good selection of English prose (it is not necessary to inflict this on an audience); and thus, while acquiring command of the refractory aspirate, the musical rhythm and balance so necessary to the quality of good English, written or spoken, will be impressed upon him.

Misuse of the letter "h" is frequently the result of failure to observe a very useful rule regarding the pronunciation of the little word "the." Before a vowel the word "the" should be pronounced as "thee"; before an "h" it should be pronounced as are the letters "th" in the word "leather." Many people invert this rule, and the result is such errors as "the hambition" and "the 'ouse."

Another common defect is the introduction of an "r" between a word which ends with a vowel and the following word which begins with a vowel—such as "the idea*r* of," and "I saw*r* an engine," etc. This fault also can be corrected by slow speaking and reading practice.

A speaker should aim continually at the extension of his vocabulary. Nevertheless, in speech, the familiar word should always be given preference over the far-fetched, the short over the long, and the concise phrase over the circumlocution.

One still finds many people with extremely hazy ideas regarding the difference in meaning and pronunciation between such words as complaisant and complacent; deprecate and depreciate; palatial and palatal; ascetic and æsthetic; veracity and voracity; allusion and illusion; proscribe and prescribe; mendacity and mendicity; principle and principal; perspicacity and perspicuity. These, and doubtless many others, will repay the looking up in a good pronouncing dictionary. You should make it a habit to hunt up every word the pronunciation or meaning of which is doubtful to you, and to continue the practice with every new word you meet. By this means your vocabulary will be increased by far more than the number of words about which you actually consult your dictionary, since each new word will supply a clue to the meanings and pronunciations of several others.

Vocabulary may be increased by any kind of reading provided it is fairly extensive. The student will be well advised, however, to apply himself more particularly to the works of really good writers (of which there is an immense and varied supply in cheap editions), for from good literature so much of great value besides vocabulary is to be gained.

In acquiring that refinement and distinction of speech associated with the best education, much assistance may be gained by joining a debating club or similar society.

You will be able to study closely the good and bad points of your fellow-members as speakers, and you will have the advantage of their probably candid criticism of yourself. In addition, the interchange of ideas will broaden your outlook and render you conversant with many new aspects of life.

Even in a small gathering of speakers you will find great diversity of style and manner of delivery. On the subject of gesture you will probably obtain considerable enlightenment. As a nation we English are extremely averse to anything in the nature of gesticulation; and the question of how to stand and what to do with one's hands is a fairly big problem to all speakers at first.

Your actions, if any, must appear absolutely spontaneous and natural. By far the best plan is to indulge in no gestures except those which *are* absolutely spontaneous and natural. In other words, restrain yourself from making any illustrative movements with your hands and arms, endeavouring to get the desired emphasis by impressive diction. When you get warmed to your subject you will probably be unable to refrain from making some gestures to drive home your points; and these, since they are quite spontaneous, will be effective.

When standing up to make a speech, assume a comfortable and easy attitude. Your hands, which may seem at first in the way, you should dispose of by clasping them behind you or resting them on a rail or chair-back—and leaving them there. (But remember, if you must put them in your pockets, to avoid jingling your money; such habits become exceedingly irritating to an audience.)

In order to be able to turn the more easily from side to side rest the weight of the body on one foot rather than on both. But do not sway from side to side continually. And do not fix your eyes upon the ground; look at your audience, though not at any particular individual.

The value of the foregoing hints will probably be well illustrated by the speakers whom you will observe at a debating club. The marring effects of certain habits, of phraseology particularly, will also present themselves to you. You will notice that the use of hackneyed quotations and expressions is somewhat displeasing ; and the following may be taken as phrases to be avoided, or at most used once only, and for a particular reason : "To be or not to be" ; "the man in the street" ; "more honoured in the breach than in the observance" ; "the light, fantastic toe" ; "the soft impeachment" ; "filthy lucre" ; "few and far between." There are many others, of course, equally threadbare.

If a quotation is to be used it is worth while to quote correctly. It is common to hear "Fresh fields and pastures new," the correct rendering of which is : "Fresh *woods* and pastures new." Another instance is, "A little knowledge is a dangerous thing" ; correctly, the phrase runs : "A little *learning* is a dangerous thing."

Certain words, too, are very often wrongly used. For instance, the verbs "to lie" and "to lay" are confused in everyday speech to an extraordinary extent. It should be remembered that the verb "to lay" is transitive—that is, a person who lays must lay *something*, as a hen or a bricklayer does. To lay *down* is a physical impossibility.

Again, archaic and obsolete words have no merit in themselves, and are liable to strike a listener as an affectation. "Yclept," "whilom," "methinks," "behest," "peradventure"—to quote a few examples—are not in keeping with modern speech, and they are, moreover, open to misapprehension.

Care should be taken also to avoid finishing a sentence with a preposition or other insignificant word. A professor of English is credited with having said that "a preposition is the one word which you must not end a sentence *with*," thus, perhaps unintentionally, doubly emphasizing his point. Such a sentence has a weak, ragged, incomplete effect. "What subject are you speaking on ?" lacks the finished, rounded form of "On what subject are you speaking ?"

The question of the use of slang may occur here, and,

whilst it would be too much to aver that slang should never be used, it must be pointed out that only in certain circumstances is it in any way effective or desirable. To some audiences, quite possibly, your arguments will be much more comprehensible and forcible if couched in the language which they themselves affect. Under such circumstances some slang may perhaps be permissible; but it should be borne in mind that the English language, wielded properly, is capable of expressing practically any idea without becoming in any way obscure, and that slang is usually the outcome of a limited vocabulary. When speaking on sporting subjects, of course, sporting slang may be used, and cannot be objected to unless it is overworked. In any case, it is a good plan to use slang sparingly. This rule ensures that if, and when, resorted to, a slang expression becomes particularly trenchant.

Metaphor and allegory are adopted to picture an idea the more vividly. In all figurative speech the image chosen should be suited to the subject, and the metaphor must be consistent throughout. By this it is not meant to debar a speaker from using a succession of apt metaphors.

The use of Latin tags and foreign phrases cannot be commended. It is true that there are some abstractions that can be expressed only with difficulty in English, and for which it is often advantageous to employ a foreign idiom. But such expedients will but rarely assist you in making your meaning clear to an average audience; and, generally, they will conclude you are airing your knowledge. And it is well to bear in mind that an effort to show off learning often results in an exposure of ignorance.

Your object as a speaker should be to say what you have to say so as to instruct or persuade your hearers; and with this end in view, your keynote should be simplicity.

It is perhaps impossible to recapitulate this rather discursive chapter after the manner adopted in the opening one; but the student will profit if he keeps in mind the importance of (1) slow reading aloud as an aid to correct use of the aspirate; (2) regular reference to a good dictionary as a means to extended vocabulary and correct pronunciation; (3) intellectual conversation and reading as methods of broadening the mind; and (4) simplicity of language and gesture as the foundation of effective style.

CHAPTER IV

THE CHAIRMAN AND HIS DUTIES

THE success of a meeting depends, in a considerable measure, on the capabilities of the chairman. We might almost claim that it succeeds or fails according to his abilities. If he is a man of farseeing qualities, possesses tact, and can discriminate without hesitation between good and bad, then the gathering over which he presides will be fortunate in its leader. If, on the other hand, the chairman is apt to vacillate, is weak in keeping order, and does not marshal the speakers properly, the meeting will then fail, in a large measure, in its purpose.

The chief duty of a chairman is to conduct the meeting, to see that all sides have a fair hearing, and to close the debates when no useful purpose will be served in letting them run on. But as the best man present at the gathering is usually put in the chair, it is a real loss to make him direct operations and deny him the privilege of expressing his opinions or of tendering advice. Strictly speaking, he should not hold any definite views, and at formal gatherings or when discord is likely to be aroused he will be wise in taking up an impartial attitude. At more informal meetings, however, where business is of a friendly character, his advice and judgment can be put to valuable use, and there is no reason why he should not speak his mind. Under such circumstances, if he is reticent on the matter, somebody in the audience should rise and ask him to express his views. There can then be no suggestion that he is not acting impartially.

Though a chairman's first duty is to be impartial, he must, in addition, possess a large share of human understanding. It will be useless, for instance, for him to be a man with a thin skin. To lose one's temper on such occasions is fatal, and the members present will be quick to perceive any display of irritation on his part. Also, he must be capable of leading others. Some people, estimable in their way, were never born to command and they should keep out of the chair at all costs. There are certain individuals whom we have seen presiding over others who think that *leading* means *bullying*. There was never a greater mistake, and any self-respecting audience will speedily disillusion a chairman who attempts to ride rough-shod over the members present.

But though a chairman has obvious duties, it must not be thought that he alone is bound by a code of honour. Everybody present must respect his position and give way to his decisions, whether they are considered just or not. At informal gatherings it is not an unusual practice for certain members to discuss matters in an undertone, which gradually increases in intensity until it becomes a nuisance to the speaker and those who wish to hear him. On such occasions the chairman has to be repeatedly asking for silence. When such happens it is decidedly bad form and a breach of the rules of debate on the part of those who offend.

Having set out these preliminary considerations, we will now enter more definitely into the conduct of a meeting as it affects the chairman. On first taking the chair it is customary for him, before commencing his duties, to thank the members for placing their confidence in him and for the honour they have accorded him by making him their chairman. A few words on this point are quite sufficient, and they will serve to show that he is sensible to his duties and appreciates his position.

The actual business now begins, and the first item under this head consists in the reading of the minutes of the last meeting, if there be any. It is the duty of the secretary to read them. When they are read the chairman asks, "Is it your pleasure, gentlemen, that I sign these minutes as correct?" As a rule the members are only too glad to get on with the fresh work in hand and they cry in unison "Yes." The chairman then signs them and adds the date. But it occasionally happens that someone questions their accuracy and raises a point at issue. Here the chairman should be very careful, for he must permit of no other debate than one concerning the correctness of the minutes. It is not unusual for such a debate to stray away from the strict points of fact to questions of policy, and all extraneous arguments the chairman must rapidly rule out of order. If an alteration in the minutes is decided upon it must be in the form of an amendment, which the secretary will insert in the proper place, together with his initials, and not till then should the chairman add his signature. On occasions, when the business of a previous meeting was unimportant or when time is very pressing, the chairman will ask, " May I take the minutes as read ? " If the general response is one of assent he signs them and proceeds with the fresh business, which commences with the work of reading any correspondence requiring consideration.

Generally the next matter is to read the notice calling the meeting and to explain, in outline, the work to be done. The notice may be the agenda. This being accomplished, the chairman takes the first point and goes into it as fully as may be necessary. Perhaps there is someone present who is known to have special knowledge on the subject. It will speed up things if the chairman calls upon this person to tell the meeting what he knows. Such a procedure is perhaps not always in strict keeping with the rules, but it is helpful, and nobody should object. If anyone is likely to dissent, the chairman can protect himself by saying " Mr. A. can, I believe, give us valuable information on the matter. Would someone propose that he now be heard ? " After it has been proposed and seconded that Mr. A. be heard, this gentleman can speak without fear of being challenged. When he has finished, the matter is thrown open for debate.

Mr. B. now rises and gives his views. If he is an accomplished speaker he will keep to the point, but, if not, he may run away from the issue, and then the chairman must firmly ask him to keep to the point. Having set forth his opinions, he should be asked from the chair to put such opinions in the form of a motion. This he will do in as few words as possible, handing them up in writing. The chairman reads them aloud and asks if somebody will second the motion. Anyone who speaks at this juncture must do so by way of being a seconder, and no other speech is in order. If there is no seconder, the matter is then open for debate. The seconder need not necessarily make a speech; he can show his willingness to support the motion by merely raising a hand or saying, "I have great pleasure in seconding Mr. B.'s motion." Nobody may speak more than once on the same motion, except the proposer, who has a right to reply when all the other speakers have finished. This privilege is accorded him to enable him to summarize the position.

When a good number of people have discussed the motion the chairman must put the question to the vote, and so gain the collective opinion of the people present. There can be no rule as to when the voting should be done, but if talkers are few the vote is taken as soon as the last one has finished. If talkers are numerous the chairman must strike a balance between the length of the agenda and the time available for its consideration. When the time reasonably allotted to one point has been exhausted he should say something to this effect, "Well, gentlemen, you see the agenda is a long one; we have a good deal of business still before us, and I think we must now take the vote on Mr. B.'s motion."

The votes may be recorded in a number of ways—in writing, by a show of hands, by taking up an appropriate position in the hall, etc. In large gatherings it is usual to appoint tellers, who count the votes; in small meetings the chairman and secretary do the work.

Whatever the result of the motion the debate on the particular points concerned must not be reopened during the meeting. We mention this because there are people who, when they have lost, endeavour by subterfuge to reopen the matter, hoping that on a second presentation they may fare more successfully. Their plan is to twist a motion that has gone against them into a new guise and so put it up again before the meeting. Of course, the alert chairman will recognize the scheme immediately and rule it out of order.

A good deal has been argued and written about what should constitute the chairman's duty when a number of people are all anxious to speak at the same time. It is usually conceded that the member who first catches the chairman's eye should be granted the permission to speak, or it may be the member who is first to rise from his seat.

If many of the people present have an idea that the chairman is favouring certain people to the detriment of others they have a very simple remedy. One of the number rises and proposes that Mr. C. be now heard, Mr. C. being, of course, someone favourable to "the other side." A friend immediately seconds the proposal and the matter is put to the vote of the meeting. The collective vote will show whether the general mass of the people is satisfied or not with the choice of speakers.

There is no doubt that the Englishman's love of fair play is such that at most meetings the chairman has little difficulty, if he possess tact, in keeping order. But although he will seldom need to fall back on stern measures it is highly important that he should know how to act when disorder does occur. As an extreme course the chairman can declare the meeting closed, and when he has left the chair all further discussion is without value. Or he can adjourn for a definite period of time. This is usually the better plan, as to close the meeting sacrifices the whole of the occasion; to adjourn it merely loses sufficient time to enable the disorderly element to come to its senses. Another plan, which proves useful in cases where someone insists on addressing the meeting against the wishes of the chair, is for a member to propose that "The question be now put." When this proposal has been seconded and carried by the meeting the offender must give way.

Of all the people who frequent meetings and display irritating ways none is more exasperating than the man who makes a point of talking whether he has anything useful to say or not. As such people are by no means rare the chairman should be severe with them and give them plainly to understand that the meeting has no time to listen to empty platitudes.

Miscellaneous Matters.—The person who occupies the chair should be addressed always as "Mr. Chairman." When a lady takes the chair she acts as a "chairman."

The only occasion when a speaker may be interrupted is when a member rises upon a "point of order." This is a process whereby a member may charge the speaker with some act which is a breach of order. It may be insulting language, unpatriotic behaviour, or a thousand other things. The member should rise immediately the supposed offence is committed and say, "Mr. Chairman, I rise upon a point of order," and then he should add his indictment. The chairman will then look into the charge and decide according to his opinions.

Should the chairman of a meeting be absent his place is filled by the vice-chairman or deputy-chairman. When there are no such appointments someone should say, "I propose that Mr. D. takes the chair," and on there being a general show of assent Mr. D. should fill the post of temporary chairman. If the chairman arrives late, the temporarily appointed chairman will, of course, vacate the position.

CHAPTER V

THE SECRETARY AND HIS DUTIES

THE duties of a secretary, in so far as they are connected with the business of conducting a meeting, are of an exacting nature, since it is upon this official that all the clerical work devolves.

When the chairman or the committee decides that a meeting is to be called it is the secretary who sends out the necessary intimations by post, by advertising, or by any other means decided on. He arranges for the hire of a suitable hall or, in the case of small gatherings, makes plans for the business to be transacted in a friend's house. He pays certain bills, makes all sorts of inquiries, and does other matters as directed by the chairman or by the minutes of the last meeting.

In addition to all this he has to compile what is practically a history of the activities of the society or body for which he stands as secretary. All documents must be filed and preserved by him, and in very many cases he should have them in readiness at meetings for inspection and reference.

But it is with the minutes of the meetings that we are here chiefly concerned. At each meeting the secretary will sit on the platform, usually close to the chairman, and he will make notes from which the minutes can be subsequently written up. He must be very careful how he does this part of the work, since any little inaccuracy will be quickly taken up by someone or other when the minutes are read at the next meeting. All motions and amendments must be reported word for word, and, to safeguard against even slight inaccuracies, the officials will be well advised if they only accept motions and amendments in writing. The secretary will then have no difficulty in reporting them accurately.

Of course every secretary will not draw up the minutes in exactly the same way, but Sir Reginald Palgrave, in "The Chairman's Handbook," suggests that the following entries should be always included:

1. Motions in the precise form in which they are put from the chair.

2. Every such question whether withdrawn, negatived, or superseded.

3. Name of the mover of every motion.

4. Names and number of the voters, showing whether each vote given was for or against the question.

5. The names also of those present at each division who, if usage so permit, took part in the debate but abstained from voting.

6. The chairman's decisions upon matters of order and his statements of opinion regarding practice or procedure.

7. The day and hour upon which a postponed or adjourned proceeding is to be considered.

8. If a special form of notice for the transaction of business is prescribed, the fact that such notice has been given should be recorded.

With the help of the above points, outlined by Sir Reginald Palgrave, the inexperienced secretary should have no difficulty in compiling the minutes of a meeting; but as an actual specimen set of minutes may also prove useful we have drawn up the following:

A Meeting of the Dickens Debating Society was held at the Castle on Wednesday, February 12th, 1936, at 7.30 p.m.

The chair was taken by Mr. Z.

The following members were present: Messrs. A., B., C., D., etc., also Mrs. P., Q., R., and Miss S. T., etc.

The Secretary, Mr. Y., was also present.

Letters of apology for their absence were read and accepted from Mr. E. and Mr. F., the former being prevented from attending by illness and the latter from business pressure.

The notice of the Meeting was read by the Secretary.

The Minutes of a meeting held on November 15th, 1935, were read by the Secretary and signed by the Chairman;

or

The Minutes of a Meeting held on November 15th, 1935, were taken as read and signed by the Chairman.

A letter was read by the Secretary from the Local Cottage Hospital accepting the Society's offer to give a Dickens presentation on Boxing Day in the hospital.

Upon the motion of Mr. A. and seconded by Mr. B. it was resolved that the programme and other details of the presentation be entrusted to Mr. B., Miss S., and the Secretary. (Voted—40 for, 4 against.)

A long discussion then ensued regarding the growing funds of the Society in the bank, and it was moved by Mr. C. and seconded by Miss T. that £20 be expended on refurnishing the club-room.

An amendment was moved by Mr. D. and seconded by Miss S. that the sum be increased to £50; but this was rejected by the meeting.

The original motion was then put to the meeting and carried by a majority of 20 votes.

Mrs. Q. then made the complaint that the library was in a neglected condition, that certain books had been borrowed and never returned, whilst others had suffered defacement that was not ordinary wear and tear. She proposed, and Mrs. R. seconded, a motion to the effect that a committee of four be appointed to inquire into a more up-to-date system of classifying, lending, and preserving the books.

The motion was put to the vote and carried unanimously.

The meeting terminated at 10.15 p.m.

While still dealing with the office of secretary it may be well to point out that a society will save itself much trouble if it elects a man for this post who is used to clerical work and who is of methodical habits. It is manifest that a secretary must know how to write a business letter—a thing which everybody cannot do, and he must be a man who answers correspondence punctually, without putting off such things to the last minute.

In many societies the secretary and treasurer are one and the same individual. While this is not a plan to be recommended when the work is considerable, the money handled is much, and the object of the society is of a public nature, it is, nevertheless, advisable in cases where the business transacted is quite private and of a friendly character. It is advisable because the secretary is not then bothered by going to the treasurer every time a small bill has to be paid or an insignificant sum disbursed. The dual rôle, however, imposes on him a necessity of keeping a strict account to the uttermost farthing, and such accounts should be constantly audited by some duly appointed member of the society.

SUMMARY

In short, the duties of a Secretary are:

(*a*) To arrange all meetings, in conference with the Chairman, paying particular attention to ensure that they are held on suitable dates.

(*b*) To give instructions for the preparation of a suitable meeting-place.

(*c*) To send out notices of meetings to all members at least seven clear days in advance.

(*d*) To attend all meetings in person, except those of committees, which are usually optional.

(*e*) To make himself conversant with all the matters likely to be discussed at meetings, so that he may assist with his knowledge.

(*f*) At the meetings, to read the notice convening such meetings, unless the Chairman elects to do so, and to read the minutes.

(*g*) To make notes during meetings, so that he will be able to write up the minute book afterwards.

(*h*) To keep the agenda, minute and other books of the society, company, etc.

(*i*) To attend to all the correspondence.

(*j*) To make all the proper returns, as needed by the Registrar of Joint Stock Companies, when a company is concerned.

Chapter VI

LOYAL TOASTS

The King

Hints.—The toast of the King should be proposed by the chief person present; it therefore devolves on some such official as the chairman or president, or on the host. In its simplest form the usual words are "Gentlemen—the King." But the proposer may care to speak at greater length, when one of the following specimens may prove useful.

SPECIMENS

A Form Suitable for a Formal Gathering

Gentlemen,—My first duty is to give you the toast of "His Majesty the King"—a duty which is in itself an honour, and one in which I am confident of the cordial support of every one here present. There is no necessity for me to enumerate those qualities in our King which endear him to us all, and cause this simple toast to be drunk with heartfelt loyalty whenever and wherever a few Britons are gathered together. Our King in a measure represents to us the greatness of the British Empire, and the liberties and the ideals for which we all strive. The enthusiasm shown on any occasion when he appears in public confirms my opinion that deep down in the heart of every Briton, whatever his class or creed, is implanted a firm loyalty to the Throne; and in that conviction I am assured that the toast I have to propose will meet with a warm and sincere response. Gentlemen, the health of His Majesty the King!

A Form Suitable for a Charity Function

Ladies and Gentlemen,—The health of His Majesty the King, which I have now the honour to propose, is a toast assured of welcome in any gathering of Britons. But on this occasion I feel that it is doubly assured of welcome, for the reason that our cause has received great assistance from the magic of our Sovereign's name. As all of you are doubtless aware, His Majesty has generously permitted the inscription of his name at the head of our list of patrons. In this he has but given a further instance of his ever-ready sympathy with all works of charity. In our Royal Family, hospitals and philanthropic enterprises of every sort have ever found invaluable friends; and His Majesty's constant solicitude for the welfare of his poorer subjects, together with the keen interest he displays in all measures for the betterment of their conditions, stamp him as a monarch worthy of the greatest loyalty and love. I call upon you, ladies and gentlemen, to drink the health of our Patron, His Majesty the King!

A Form Suitable to a Gathering where Patriotic Sentiments are liable to be at a Discount

Ladies and Gentlemen,—My duty to-night is to propose the toast of "The King," and I approach my task not without some feelings of diffidence. In a great Empire like ours, of which we may be justly proud, whilst still conscious of its failings, I am convinced that it is necessary that we should have some official head. There may be amongst you some who may question whether the particular form of Constitution we now have is the best; but it is one that has not only weathered great crises and withstood the storm of circumstances; it is one that has been responsive to those pressures which tend to modify and improve its form. In his capacity as constitutional ruler our King has repeatedly given evidence of his willingness to be guided by the Ministers chosen by his people, and has shown that it is his desire to accommodate himself to the tendencies of our age. It is our historic tradition, perhaps, which necessitates the maintenance of the pomp and circumstance which to many may seem unnecessary; but to-day, as of old, the cry of the people is *panem et circenses*. It is for this reason that the trappings of Royalty are maintained, whilst its inward spirit, as I think, moves with the times. George the Sixth is, I believe I may truly claim, a real people's king, and a fitting representative of the great imperial race over which he presides. As head of the State he forms, as it were, a personal link between the British Isles and those great outlying and self-governing colonies spread throughout the seven seas; and it is as a symbol such as this that a king is of real value. The position of a king is one of unparalleled difficulty; his high office is not of his own choosing; his privileges and prerogatives nowadays are exercised by others in his name. His greatness, such as it is, is literally thrust upon him; and it is no more than just to say that our King, in a trying position not of his own choosing, does his very best. Therefore, ladies and gentlemen, I feel assured that, whatever your individual shades of opinion may be, you will join with me sincerely in wishing our King long life and good health!

A Form Suitable for a Gathering of Sportsmen

Gentlemen,—It is my pleasant duty now to propose the health of one of the finest sportsmen in the country. I speak of His Majesty the King. Although he has been on the Throne a comparatively short time, he has already shown, in many ways, that even the most busy man can find time for sportive recreations.

As we all know, his duties of state are arduous but, even so, we are glad to see that our King is still the dashing sportsman that he was when Duke of York. This, gentlemen, is all very much to the good for, as long as our King devotes a sensible amount of time to healthy recreations, so he will be likely to keep his strength and vigour.

As you must all realise, there are very strong temptations for Royalty to tax their energies beyond reasonable limits and, consequently, to undermine their constitutions. This, I verily believe, was what brought about the lamented death of his respected father, King George V. But as long as our present King preserves his interests in various sports and finds time to indulge in them, we need have little fear that he is killing himself for his country.

King George's favourite pastime is tennis: but he plays an excellent game of polo and is no mean exponent of golf. With a rod and line, he is far from being a novice and in swimming he is well able to hold his own. It occurs to me that when the National Playing Fields Association was started in 1925, he eagerly became its president. Gentlemen, this is a fine record of a fine sportsman.

In the hunting-field, our King has long been a well-known and popular figure; he is an excellent shot; and there is not one of our national sports with which he has not at some time or other identified himself—not merely as a patron, but as a worthy exponent. His motto through life has been "play the game", and we can rest assured that he will play the game until his dying day. I ask you, then, gentlemen, to be upstanding and drink the health of that real sportsman, "His Majesty the King."

A Form Suitable for General Occasions

Ladies and Gentlemen,—At a gathering of such a character as this it would be impossible for us to pass to the consideration of other toasts before the one which every loyal Englishman and Englishwoman must agree is an honour to propose. It is our happy fortune to live in a country with a Constitution which has served as a model to other great nations and peoples of the world; and the head of this great Constitution is one to whom we can honestly look, I think, with admiration and respect—

if not reverence—by reason of his proved ability to give the right lead to the people over whom it has been destined that he should preside. It would be needless for me to remind you of the many occasions on which our noble Sovereign and his gracious Queen have exhibited those royal qualities which, whilst we may expect to find them, have not been shown invariably by our monarchs in the past. The personal consideration which His Majesty has ever displayed towards even the humblest of his subjects, and the oft-manifested sympathy of the Queen, need no words of mine to embellish. As the Duke of York, he had the advantage of his father's admirable guidance. He grew up with a charm of personality to sturdy manhood, and his excellent qualities have completely won our love and respect. I, therefore, ask you to fill your glasses and drink to the continued long life, well-being, and prosperity of the King, the Queen, and the other members of the Royal Family.

USEFUL QUOTATIONS

May the King live ever in the hearts of his subjects.

Whoever is King is also father of his country.—*Congreve.*

A good king is a public servant.—*Ben Jonson.*

Kings will be tyrants from policy, when subjects are rebels from principle.—*Burke.*

Our Country! In her intercourse with foreign nations may she always be in the right, but Our Country, right or wrong.

All government is an evil, but of the two forms of that evil, democracy or monarchy, the sounder is monarchy.—
"Table Talk."

Nothing appears more surprising to those who consider human affairs with a philosophical eye, than the easiness with which the many are governed by the few.—*Hume.*

As the Government is, such will be the man—*Plato.*

Special Note.—It is interesting to note that Lancastrian and Cornish people have a special privilege when giving the toast of The King, which others are denied. The correct form in their case is to say "The King, Duke of Lancaster" or "The King, Duke of Cornwall," as the case may be. This form of submitting the toast has been given official sanction. The instructions proceed to point out that for Lancastrians to toast The King as "The Duke of Lancaster" is wrong, and similarly for Cornish people to toast him as "The Duke of Cornwall."

The double form of toast is only allowed officially, to people residing in the respective counties or at gatherings of the County Associations held outside the Counties. In all other cases, "The King," without additions should be uttered.

These forms hold for such time as The King retains the title to the two dukedoms. If successors are appointed, the simple form of the toast is reverted to.

THE KING—BIOGRAPHICAL NOTES

Albert Frederick Arthur George—Second son of King George V. and Queen Mary: born at York Cottage, Sandringham, December 14, 1895.

Married Lady Elizabeth Bowes-Lyon, April 26, 1923. Has two children, H.R.H. Princess Elizabeth (born April 21, 1926) and H.R.H. Princess Margaret Rose (born August 21, 1930).

Entered R. Naval College, Osborne, January 1909, and then proceeded to Dartmouth.

Midshipman on the H.M.S. *Collingwood*, 1913.

Sub-lieutenant in the Battle of Jutland, 1916.

Wing Commander in Royal Air Force, 1920.

Created Duke of York, 1920.

Opened the Houses of Parliament, Canberra, Australia, May 1927.

Ascended the throne, December 11, 1936.

Crowned, May 12, 1937.

Her Majesty The Queen

Hints.—As a general rule, the toast to the Queen is embodied in either the toast to the King, or to the Royal Family. There are occasions, however, when an individual toast to Her Majesty is desirable—see the hints which precede the specimen toast to the Royal Family, on the next page.

SPECIMEN

Ladies and Gentlemen,—I trust you all have your glasses charged, for it is now my privilege to propose to you the health of Her Majesty the Queen. Though I look upon the duty which devolves on me as a great honour, I am fully conscious of the difficulties. It is no easy matter to speak of Her Majesty in adequate terms.

The Queen, whether you think of her as a wife, a mother or the First Lady of the Land, you cannot but admit that she possesses a dignity and a charm which call for our respect and esteem. Her many qualities provide us with a pattern well worthy of imitation. You will agree with me, I am sure, when I say that the country is fortunate in possessing such a Queen.

From the highest subject to the lowest, there is a personal feeling of regard towards this gracious lady. To every one of us, she is something more than our Queen. It is really very difficult to define exactly the position she holds in our hearts, but I am sure everyone of us knows the feeling to which I am alluding.

Many of us in this room lead busy lives and many of us find that each day is all too short for the work that has to be crammed into it. But compared with the duties of Her Majesty, ours seem trifling. What with state functions, social duties and family cares, her life is more than fully occupied. Yet, with it all, she manages to take a lively interest in a thousand and one activities which touch the hearts of her subjects and, what is more, she invariably has a smile and a pleasant word for those who come within her presence.

[Refer here to any particular matters which connect the present function to Her Majesty's name.]

And now, Ladies and Gentlemen, I ask you to be upstanding and to drink to the health of our beloved Queen.

THE ROYAL FAMILY

Hints,—It is the usual practice to propose the health of the King, intending it to serve not only for him but for all the members of the Royal Family. This plan is not always satisfactory when special conditions are at issue. Then the custom is first to speak of the King and to follow with the toast of the members of the Royal Family in a second speech. This arrangement is always departed from when one of the members of the Royal Family is present or is specially concerned. Then a toast devoted to the particular member is proposed after that of the King.

SPECIMEN

Ladies and Gentlemen,—I count myself particularly favoured, to-night, in being entrusted with the toast of the Royal Family. It is a toast which I am sure you will all welcome in a warm and cordial manner, since we all have a very kindly regard for the members of the Royal Family. I am glad that the Chairman has separated this toast from that of the King, because as you know it is the practice in some quarters to drink to the health of "the King and the rest of the Royal Family." This was done on one occasion when Edward VII was the then Prince of Wales. The noble Prince immediately rose and said he begged leave to state that there was no rest for the Royal Family. That, ladies and gentlemen, is the true position! there is no rest for the Royal Family. If ever a family worked consistently hard, without a word of grumble and with no thought but that of the general good, it is our Royal Family. Some wise person once said that a country has the Royalty it deserves. If this is true, we have every reason to congratulate ourselves. In my own time, I have seen several Royal Houses forced to leave their countries—Spain, Portugal, Germany. That is something that will never happen in the British Isles as long as Britain is Britain. Ladies and gentlemen, I give you the toast, "the Royal Family."

USEFUL QUOTATIONS

Titles, instead of exalting, debase those who act not up to them.—*La Rochefoucauld.*

Nothing is more binding than the friendship of companions-in-arms.—*Hillard.*

Pleasure is far sweeter as a recreation than as a business.
—*Hitchcock.*

I find the Englishman to be him of all men who stands firmest in his shoes.—*Emerson.*

Example is more efficacious than precept.—*Johnson.*

THE ROYAL FAMILY—BIOGRAPHICAL NOTES

H.M. King George VI.—see page 41.

H.M. Queen Elizabeth.—Born at Glamis Castle, Aug. 4., 1900.—(see p. 41.)

H.R.H. Princess Elizabeth.—see page 41.

H.R.H. Princess Margaret Rose.—see page 41.

H.M. Queen Mary.—Born at Kensington Palace, May 26, 1867. Eldest child of the Duke of Teck. Great-granddaughter of George III. Married, July 6, 1893. Of H.M.

Queen Mary, it has been said that "she possesses the dignity required by her position and a manner graciously correct, though never frigid."

H.R.H. the Duke of Windsor.—First son of King George V. Born at White Lodge, Richmond Park, June 23, 1894.

H.R.H. The Princess Royal (Victoria Alexandra Alice Mary).—Only daughter of King George V. Born April 25, 1897. Married Viscount Lascelles, now the Earl of Harewood, Feb. 28, 1922. Has two sons, George, Viscount Lascelles (born, Feb. 7, 1923) and Hon. Gerald Lascelles (born, Aug. 21, 1924).

H.R.H. The Duke of Gloucester.—Third son of King George V. Born March 31, 1900. Married Lady Alice Scott, daughter of the Duke of Buccleuch, Nov. 6, 1935.

H.R.H. The Duke of Kent.—Fourth son of King George V. Born Dec. 20, 1902. Married H.R.H. Princess Marina of Greece, Nov. 29, 1934. Has two children, Edward (born, Oct. 9, 1935) and Alexandra (born, Dec. 25th, 1936).

H.R.H. The Duke of Connaught.—Brother of King Edward VII. Born May 1, 1850. Married H.R.H. Princess Louisa of Prussia, March 13, 1879 (The Princess died March 14, 1917).

H.R.H. Prince Arthur of Connaught.—Son of the above. Born Jan. 13, 1883. Married the Duchess of Fife, Oct. 15, 1913.

H.R.H. Princess Patricia (Lady Patricia Ramsay).—Daughter of the Duke of Connaught. Born March 17, 1886. Married Sir Alexander Ramsay, Feb. 27, 1919.

H.R.H. Princess Louise.—Daughter of Queen Victoria. Born March 18, 1848. Married the Marquess of Lorne (afterwards 9th Duke of Argyll) March 21, 1871.

H.R.H. Princess Beatrice.—Daughter of Queen Victoria. Born April 14, 1857. Married H.R.H. Prince Henry of Battenberg July 23, 1885. The Prince died Jan. 20, 1896.

H.R.H. Princess Maud, Queen of Norway.—Sister of King George V. Born Nov. 26, 1869. Married King Haakon VII, July 22, 1896.

His Majesty's Forces

The Royal Navy

Hints.—There must, of course, be a patriotic ring about this speech. No one who does not feel in entire sympathy with the matter should propose it. Allusions to historical and technical data will help to enliven the discourse but this must be done sparingly. Some of the following facts may prove useful:

England's Navy first established by Alfred, A.D. 896.

First "Dreadnought," 1907.

Oil fuel first used by Admiralty, 1900.

Submarines first built for Admiralty, 1902.

Drake (1540–1596).—Beat the Spanish Armada.

Raleigh (1552–1618).—Discovered new lands in America, made Virginia an English colony, assisted in defeat of the Armada. Executed by King James I.

Rodney (1718–1792).—Fought the Spaniards and relieved Gibraltar. Fought a number of successful engagements while suffering from gout, and gave his orders while sitting in a chair.

Nelson (1758–1805).—Many successes against the French, notably Trafalgar. Died of wounds in action and body brought home preserved in brandy. Several sailors abstracted and drank some of the spirit; they were given eighty lashes. Last words, "Thank God, I have done my duty."

SPECIMEN

(Proposed by the chairman)

Gentlemen,—I now have the honour to propose the toast of that "silent Service," the Navy. It may well be silent, I think, since its deeds have ever spoken for themselves. If History counts for anything, we may all be proud of the part the Navy has played in shaping our destinies. From the Armada to Jutland, it has provided one long unbroken list of successes; and throughout, it has guarded our shores and kept them inviolate. What deeds of skill and valour are conjured up by such names as Drake, Hood, Howe, Nelson and, in our own times, Beatty and Jellicoe! There have been moments when we have wondered whether the Navy could cope with the forces massed against it. But our fears—if fears they were—have been groundless, for on each and every occasion, our ships have come out on top. Of old we spoke of ships of oak and hearts of oak. Nowadays our ships are of steel; and it is not too much to say that the staunchness of our sailormen has evolved in a like manner with their ships. Naught but iron courage and nerves of steel can stand the strain of naval warfare to-day; our sailors are veritable men of steel! Our Navy is an institution of which we can be more justifiably proud to-day than ever before; therefore, gentlemen, I count on an enthusiastic response to my toast to the Empire's sure shield—the Navy!

USEFUL QUOTATIONS

To the tar who sticks like pitch to his enemies.

Hearts of oak even though iron-clad.

A new recruit on putting to sea and suffering with sickness said afterwards that for the first day he was afraid he would die and the second day he was afraid he wouldn't.

Britain's sheet anchor—her ships.

The best thing I know between France and England is the sea.—*Jerrold.*

The Army

Hints.—This, also, must be a patriotic speech, breathing the spirit of England's glorious past. Allusions to historical and technical data will help to enliven the speech, but the discourse must not be a schoolroom lesson dealing with the Army. Some of the following facts may be threaded into the wording:

Alexander (356–323 B.C.).—Conquered most of the then known world.

Cæsar (100–44 B.C.).—The greatest of all Roman generals. Invaded Britain, 55 B.C.

Alfred the Great (849–901).—One of England's greatest soldiers. Did not burn the cakes, in spite of the history books.

William the Conqueror (1027–1087).—Conquered England and set it on a more civilized footing.

Cromwell (1599–1658).—As able in politics as in military prowess.

Napoleon (1769–1821).—Too ambitious to be entirely successful.

Wellington (1769–1852).—Very calm and far seeing. Greatest success was Waterloo. Known as the "Iron Duke."

SPECIMEN

(Proposed by the chairman)

Gentlemen,—The next toast on our list is that of the Army. It is with particular pleasure that I rise to propose it, for, although I myself have never had the honour of serving my country as a soldier, my near forbears and descendants have almost all done so. Britain has ever been proud of its Army and it has abundant reason for being so. Here and there, history records that other countries have seen fit to speak disparagingly of "the thin red line." Gentlemen, there has never been an occasion when those who made such remarks have not had ample opportunities of revising their opinions. I can quote a score of instances when this has happened, if chapter and verse is needed. But what to me is the most marvellous feature of our Army is that its efficiency, equalled by no other army in the world, has been brought about although nobody could accuse us of being a military-minded nation. We do not preach militarism; we do not grow up to think in terms of guns and bullets; we do not force our entire manhood to form fours on the barrack square. But, without fuss and noise, we have an Army, the quality of which is the admiration and, in many cases, the envy of the world. Gentlemen, "The British Army."

USEFUL QUOTATIONS

The thin red line.

Firm in disaster, courageous in danger, and generous in victory.

Honour the sword.

May good leaders ever have good followers.

War never leaves where it found a nation.—*Burke.*

The commonwealth of Venice in their armoury have this inscription: "Happy is that city which in time of peace thinks of war."—*Burton.*

There never was a good war or a bad peace.—*Franklin.*

Terrible as is war, it yet displays the spiritual grandeur of man daring to defy his mightiest hereditary enemy—Death.

The great acts of war require to be undertaken by noblemen.—*Hugo.*

Nothing except a battle lost can be half so melancholy as a battle won.—*Duke of Wellington.*

The Royal Air Force

Hints.—This toast should be treated on the lines suggested for the Navy and Army. In order that the speaker may have some salient facts that may be useful for incorporation in his oration, we append the following:

The R.A.F., formed by the amalgamation of the Royal Naval Air Service and the Royal Flying Corps, 1917, is administered by the Air Ministry. In addition, there is the Fleet Air Arm which is now administered by the Navy.

In 1935, there were fifty-one regular and thirteen auxiliary squadrons in Great Britain, eight in India, four in Iraq, six in Egypt and Palestine, one at Aden and two at Singapore. The Air estimates for 1935 were £25,985,000.

The Air Force Cross, instituted in 1918, is awarded to officers for acts of courage or devotion to duty when flying, not necessarily in the presence of the enemy.

The Distinguished Flying Cross, instituted in 1918, is awarded to officers as above, but in the presence of the enemy.

The Air Force Medal and the Distinguished Flying Medal are awarded as above, but to warrant and non-commissioned officers and men.

SPECIMEN

(Proposed by the chairman)

Gentlemen,—The toast it is now my duty to propose is a comparatively new one. In the days prior to the war what little "Air Force" we had formed a component part of the Army. In the short space of a few years the infant has outgrown its parent, and now stands alone—a worthy descendant, with characteristics entirely its own. It has a future before it of unbounded possibilities; already it has a tradition as great and glorious, if not as old, as that of any other fighting force. It has produced heroes in no small number—Ball, McCudden, Bishop, are names that will never sink into oblivion. The records of the old Royal Flying Corps and Naval Air Service show a spirit of youthful daring and energy without which the present Air Force could never have come into being, and which forms the keynote of that esprit de corps which pervades this new Service to-day. It is a young Service; its ways are those of all youthful things—energetic, forceful, and greatly daring. Doubtless this impetuosity requires some measure of restraint. But I would remind you that without it the marvellous advancements being made in aerial science would be impossible. We raise our hats to our pilots, who are the finest in the world; and we salute all those whose work lies less in view. I am alluding to the men who work on the ground and who prepare the way for those who do the actual flying. The Royal Air Force is a Service which, in spite of its novelty, has nobly earned a right to our esteem; it has achieved great things, and will, I am confident, achieve greater. Charge your glasses, then, gentlemen, and drink a bumper toast to the Royal Air Force, offspring of the Army and Navy—a worthy child of worthy parents!

USEFUL QUOTATIONS

Per ardua ad astra.

Nicknames—the "Hawks"; also the "Sky Pilots."

May British laurels never fade.

War is nothing more than a reflection or image of the soul. It is the fiend within coming out.—*Channing.*

Heroism is the self-devotion of genius manifesting itself in action.—*Hare.*

In a truly heroic life there is no peradventure. It is always either doing or dying.—*Hitchcock.*

If necessity breeds no heroism, the people are not worth their own redemption.—*Mazzini.*

If silence is ever golden, it must be at the graves of men whose lives were more significant than speech, and whose death was a poem, the music of which can never be sung.
—*Garfield.*

His Majesty's Forces

(A Toast combining all three of the regular fighting arms)

SPECIMEN

Gentlemen.—Having drunk to the health of His Majesty and the other respected members of the Royal Family, I rise to propose the toast of the Navy, the Army and the Air Force. Sometimes, these three forces are taken separately and each is accorded its own toast: but here it is the intention to deal with them as a whole. Gentlemen, do not think that this is done in any slighting way.

Just as they combine, when war is afoot, to gain the strength which comes of unity, so we are combining them for a similar purpose; and when you stand and raise your glasses, let it be with a triple sense of pride and gratefulness.

I say "with pride and gratefulness." Yes, gentlemen, we are proud of our fighting forces and we are grateful to them. I ask you, what has kept certain countries, in recent times, from invading our shores or stealing parts of our Empire? It was certainly not the talks and the pacts that were indulged in at Geneva, Locarno and other places I could mention. Mind you, I am not saying that talks and treaties are not good in their way. But, what I do say is that no amount of talking will convince some of our rebellious neighbours, unless there is force behind it. And, the Navy, the Army and the Air Force provide the backing which our statesmen need when they hold conferences in various corners of the Continent.

I am rather afraid that some people take too much for granted. They have read their history books and become satiated with the succession of victories which our men have gained. And because victory after victory has been won, they have ceased to marvel at the glorious and brilliant record which our men have put up for close on a thousand years. To me, it is an astonishing and marvellous record, unparalleled by that of any other country.

For one thing I am deeply grateful. I know something of the efficiency of our forces as it is to-day and, I can assure you that if ever we ought to be proud of the Navy, the Army and the Air Force, we ought to be to-day. Gentlemen, I charge you to stand upright and drink proudly to His Majesty's Forces.

Our Noble Selves

(A Toast to a particular Regiment, Battery, or Squadron)
(Proposed by the chairman)

Hints.—See foregoing under Navy, Army, etc.

SPECIMEN

Gentlemen,—I now rise to propose the toast of the evening, —— Squadron, the Royal ——. We have assembled here this evening with the primary intention of honouring, in our own way, the name of the old unit in which we have all, at one time or another, served. There can be few here who had earlier acquaintance with —— Squadron than myself. I saw many fresh faces come, remain for a while, and then depart for other spheres of activity. Several of those faces I am glad and proud to see here to-night. Some there were amongst my old friends and comrades who have since made the supreme sacrifice; in making that sacrifice they have but borne their part in upholding and fashioning the glorious traditions which it has ever been our pride to maintain. But those who have passed out would be the last to wish us to be gloomy on an occasion such as this. What greater delight is there for old warriors than the fighting of old battles over again—with the aid of good wine and the fragrant weed? Need I remind you of the strenuous days we passed at —— during the——? We earned there a reputation that made us the envy of our neighbours and rivals, the Royal ——. Need I speak of the great night we had when the news came through that ——'s great deed had earned him the soldier's most coveted reward? No; I see by your faces that the old memories glow within you yet. As a soldier is taught to do, I regard —— Squadron as the finest unit in His Majesty's Forces; I am confident that its present members will never allow its glorious past to be forgotten; I am confident they will add to its already great list of achievements; and, finally, and above all, I am supremely confident that with enthusiasm and one accord you will drink with me to the continued honour of —— Squadron, the Royal ——'s!

USEFUL QUOTATIONS

See under Navy, Army, etc.

The Territorials

Hints.—Territorial dinners are frequently held and then this toast becomes an important one. In addition, it is not uncommon for the Territorials to be toasted at dinners that are of a purely social character. On such occasions, it usually happens that the body of people organising the dinner have a strong muster of Territorials among them, and they rightly feel the fact should be emphasised and suitably acknowledged.

SPECIMEN

(Proposed by somebody not in the Territorials)

Gentlemen,—On occasions such as these, it seems to be the invariable custom for the speaker to preface his remarks by stating that he wished the task had been entrusted to worthier and more capable hands. I am no exception to the rule, for while I have the utmost regard for this fine body of men, I do feel that I am lamentably ignorant of some of the salient facts connected with their organisation. But, however ignorant I may be, it must be and is evident to all of us, who might be described as outsiders, that the Territorial Army is composed of men whose first thought is the safety of their country.

Gentlemen, there can be no finer motive than this and I know you will bear it in mind when I call upon you to raise your glasses. In many ways, the Territorial Army is the Cinderella service of our defences. I may be wrong, but the impression I have is that its efficiency is maintained in spite of the control at the top. The Government offers little incentive that it should be carried on at full strength and full efficiency, and were it not for the patriotic actions of those concerned, I fear we should have no Territorial Army in a very short while. That, gentlemen, would be a calamity, as we all must realize if we remember the happenings of the past.

In this room, we have (*names, if not too numerous*). All these gentlemen devote a large portion of their leisure to the cause. They give up their Saturdays, a large part of their evenings and a good slice of their annual holidays in order that they may do their bit in maintaining the defences of the country. Their conception of duty is a grand one, for they are not in any doubt as to what would be required of them were this fair land to be plunged once more into another ghastly conflict.

Therefore, I ask you, gentlemen, to drink to the health of the Territorial Army. And with this toast, I beg leave to couple the names of—— and ——. (*These two gentlemen will be called upon to make the reply.*)

Reply to the Toast of The Royal Navy

SPECIMEN

Gentlemen,—I thank you for the very cordial way in which you rose and drank to the toast of the Navy. I need hardly tell you that the efficiency of the Fleet is the greatest factor for peace which this country possesses. It must be perfectly obvious to all, that Britain has no aggressive intention; and it is equally obvious that she has no desire to restrict the legitimate operations of any other country. At the same time, it is our bounden duty to maintain the Fleet in a state of efficiency, not against any danger to be seen, but against the possibility of an unforeseen danger.

For this reason, the time came when a thorough overhauling of our ships and equipment was called for. During 1914–18 our ships were worn out far more rapidly than they would have been in time of peace; and since 1918, we have depended more on treaties and talks than on the provision of new material. We, however, reached a point when it would have been suicidal to go any further. This fact, coupled with the increasing fleets of other countries throughout the world, made it imperative that we should raise our sea power to a more equitable standard.

A programme of replacements has been drawn up and I am sure every whole-hearted Briton supports the Admiralty in its efforts to safeguard the country. Let me state very clearly that there is no question of a new campaign of rivalry with other countries. We intend no more than to bring the Fleet to a condition of efficiency that will lift it above the danger line. Gentlemen, I thank you.

Reply to the Toast of The Army

SPECIMEN

Gentlemen,—I wish to thank you very sincerely for the spirited words which have been uttered about the Army and for the way you have accepted the toast. Although I am an army-man, born and bred so to speak in a red coat, I think you will allow me to say that there is no soldier in the world to beat a British Tommy, and there is no army in the world to equal the British Army, if you leave out the question of numbers. This may sound egoistic and you may say that it is self-praise. But, having spent my life in the Army, I should be in a good position to judge and I can assure you that these are the true facts.

I definitely do not want to say anything about the dark days of 1914–18; most of us try to forget them; but if there is any question of these facts, I can quote you a thousand instances to prove what I contend is right.

To-day, we do not hear a great deal about military matters. The papers are giving us a rest. But, please do not take this to mean that the Army is resting on its laurels, or that it is asleep. You may take it from me that it is very much alive. It was never so efficient as it is at the moment. In every possible way, it is being mechanised and being brought up-to-date. The standards of even ten years ago would not be tolerated for a moment to-day. So you may lie in your beds in comfort and gain satisfaction from the knowledge that Tommy Atkins is very much alive.

In only one way could the Army be improved. It is too small for the country's needs and ought to be brought up to a fuller strength. I know that I am now treading on dangerous ground and some will disagree with me. But, having thrown out the hint, I will leave it at that. Gentlemen, before sitting down, let me thank you once more for the kind way you have welcomed the toast. Thank you.

Reply to the Toast of The Royal Air Force

SPECIMEN

Mr. Chairman and Gentlemen,—I feel I am quite unworthy of the honour that has been conferred upon me. I am far too young a member of the Air Force to take upon my immature shoulders the task of replying, on behalf of the great Service of which I am so insignificant a part, to your enthusiastically expressed goodwill towards us. Perhaps my youthfulness was the cause of our worthy chairman's remarks on the youthful and impetuous spirit of the Force! Be that as it may, I am not going to deny the truth of his remarks; but I would like to add my quota to what he also said in regard to the vast amount of hum-drum routine work which we are called upon to perform. I know that we have a reputation for being rather a hare-brained, dare-devil crowd of young scamps. I even heard it said the other day that that same irresponsible spirit pervaded even that awe-inspiring institution called the

Air Ministry, and that it was responsible for the reckless finance, etc., with which that body had been credited. But I would like to dispute the accusation. We are not so bad as we have been painted—not nearly so rash and impetuous as some would have you believe. Really, we are extremely cautious! For those who lack caution, I would remind you, do not last long in our profession! But, jesting on one side, I must say, gentlemen, that I feel greatly honoured by the way in which you have expressed your appreciation of the Service to which I belong; and, as a humble member of that Service, I beg leave to return heartfelt thanks, on behalf of the Royal Air Force, for your generous expression of good feeling.

USEFUL QUOTATIONS

See under Navy, Army, etc.

Reply to the Toast of His Majesty's Forces

SPECIMEN

Gentlemen.—It is with a sense of pleasure and pride that I listened to the speech which Mr.—— has just rendered. I thank you all very cordially, on behalf of His Majesty's Forces, for the way you welcomed the toast and I am grateful to Mr. —— for his generous words. Believe me, when I say that I much appreciate the way you have seen fit to combine the three forces and honour them as one whole. Though the Navy, the Army and the Air Force are three separate entities, their common aim is the same—to guard the Mother Country and the Empire, and, on occasions such as this, they welcome the unity of spirit which you have shown. Let me tell you that though there is plenty of rivalry between the three forces, it is a friendly rivalry, and nobody who has not the privilege of being a member of one of them can really know how strong the bond of affection existing between the three actually is.

I trust, Gentlemen, that when you stood and did honour to us so wholeheartedly, you not only thought of the forces at home but that your memories wandered back to the days when the sailors and soldiers of our Colonial Empire were rallying to the call of the Motherland. These Colonial forces, it must be understood, are a very real part of our fighting strength and no estimate of our martial prowess is complete without them.

And, do not let us think only of the regular forces. The Reserves and the Auxiliaries, the Territorials and the O.T.C's, they must all share in this appreciation of yours to-night. Really, I raise my hat to these men who, while following their peaceful avocations, find time for martial training.

Gentlemen, I will detain you no longer. You have honoured us to-night very cordially, and I thank you.

Reply to the Toast of The Territorials

SPECIMEN

Gentlemen,—I have listened with very great satisfaction to all that has been said about the Territorials and I thank you very sincerely. Of course, being one of them, I am perhaps a little biased in favour of this civilian unit of the Army. It is my belief that every young man ought to ask himself very seriously whether he ought not to join up.

You will notice that I do not say that every young man ought to join. I know that many of them could not spare the time and some have not the right temperament. But I do say that every young man ought to consider the question, in so far as it affects himself.

For those who join, there is plenty of hard work; but it is interesting work. Moreover, it is healthy work and, if the lighter side be considered, I may say that it has been the means, in my case, of making a whole host of excellent friends. I look round the room and I see several of those friends here now. I trust they, also, have gained good friends by their connection with the "Terriers."

Of course, there are many people—some of them quite intelligent—who wonder what exactly the Territorials do and what they are worth in times of emergency. The Territorials go through a course of military training which would make them very valuable men, if another war came along. By that, please do not think that any one in the Territorial or even the Regular Army wants a war. Their motto is "To prepare is to prevent" and that is why they are so keen on their self-imposed task.

I will detain you no longer, but will thank you all once more for the very hearty way you accepted the toast. Gentlemen, I thank you.

His Majesty's Ministers

The following are two specimen speeches which will prove valuable as they are actual examples. They are abridged from a report in "The Times" and were delivered at a Royal Academy banquet held at Burlington House.

The President, proposing the toast of "His Majesty's Ministers," said: The Royal Academy could have no politics, or, at least, no party politics; so whoever might be in office at the time were warmly welcomed on those occasions, for they knew that they must be good men and true, all possessed with one object and intent—to carry the burden of their great responsibility so as to promote the higher development of the mind, body, and estate of all sections of the people. (Cheers.) It was a particular pleasure to them to have at their table the head of the Government—for it was some years since they had been honoured by the presence of a Prime Minister. It almost seemed that when the present Prime Minister was in evidence there came into the political atmosphere "an ampler ether, a diviner air." A short time ago, when Mr. Baldwin in the House of Commons made that noble appeal to what was best in man, so that what was best could be for the State, one felt that a region had been gained beyond political strife where the extremist might cease from troubling and the patriot be at rest. (Cheers.)

REPLY BY THE PREMIER (MR. BALDWIN)

I understand these are friendly gatherings at which confidences may be given and exchanged, and I should like to tell you something of the difficulties of a Prime Minister's life. A Prime Minister has to form a Cabinet. I reflected when I was making mine that I should have to appear to-night at Burlington House, and I thought the greatest compliment I could pay the Academy would be to include if possible a painter in the Cabinet. I thought I would choose someone who could paint with a broad brush—(laughter)—and I regret extremely that he, at the last moment, had to cancel his engagement here to-night. I need hardly say I refer to the Chancellor of the Exchequer. (Laughter.) When I had secured my artist, the question was where to put him. I at once decided that the right place for him was where he would have problems to solve of currency and exchanges and where he would be dealing with mathematics. (Laughter.) Many of my critics were hostile, but they were not astonished. If they had known their Plato they would have known at once why I asked him to go to the Exchequer. Many here will remember what Plato said to the Delians. When the oracle set a problem Plato said, "It must be supposed not that the god specially wished this problem solved, but that he would have the Greeks desist from war and wickedness and cultivate the Muses, so that, their passions being assuaged by philosophy and mathematics, they might live in innocent and mutually helpful intercourse with one another." (Laughter.) It is an extraordinary thing how the solution of many of our difficulties was really found many years ago. (Laughter.)

Now I said there were many points of resemblance between your careers and ours. Neither artists nor politicians can by any figure of speech be said to belong to organized labour. Labour, yes; organized, no. (Laughter.) What power have we to strike? (Laughter.) If every artist in this country laid down his brush to-night, would a ripple pass over the country? If I laid down my brush to-night, are there not fifty men who would be ready to take it up? But then, on the other hand, you cannot be nationalized, and neither can we. (Laughter.) It is sometimes to your advantage, and sometimes the advantage rests with us. Now take criticism. We both either suffer or enjoy criticism. There I think the advantage is with us. (Laughter.) We, if we think fit, can answer back. These canvases on the walls have to take it in contemptuous silence. (Laughter.) Your instruments by which you work so well are dumb—pencils and paints. Ours are neither dumb nor inert. (Laughter.) I often think that we rather resemble Alice in Wonderland, who tried to play croquet with a flamingo instead of a mallet.

Then, again, with both of us, to achieve success it is necessary to mix our colours, so as to produce a harmonious whole. But your colours have an advantage over those which are mixed on our palette. In the language of the trade, your colours are fast; ours are not necessarily. You mix your colours to form a harmonious result, but it may be after four or five years some of the colours which you thought the most beautiful have faded, and have been unable to stand the bright light of day, and those which you thought mixed well in the general scheme have come up hard and crude and dominate the whole picture. We politicians are, and must of necessity be, impressionists—impressionists, because we want to catch the public eye, and we hope that we can make our meaning clear. We also trust—my colleagues and I—that people will not examine our workmanship too closely lest they find defects in it which are not visible at a distance. (Laughter.) But there is one thing in which you have a great advantage. If when you complete a piece of work you do not like it, you can put your boot through it. With us the boot is on the other leg. (Laughter.)

I have noticed sometimes that advice is given to the artists of this country to make a clean sweep of the Academy. It is always a revolutionary people who think a clean sweep must result in something which will give keen satisfaction. While, in the last four years, the Academy has remained without great change, we have made a clean sweep of three Governments, and we have a fourth in—and yet people are not satisfied. (Laughter.) So may there not be something said even for keeping an Academy or keeping a Government in? (Laughter.)

There is one thing that we do have in common. No man in politics can ever hope to achieve his desire—he can never accomplish the veriest fragment of what he would will to do. In the same way, in the breast of every artist who is an artist—and it is not everyone who uses a brush who is an artist—there is a secret known only to himself and spoken of to none—that ideal which he is ever seeking and ever following up and never in this world captures. It is that which drives men on to their best and finest work. I doubt if any real artist has ever satisfied himself. Occasionally, there comes what Kipling has called the "magic," whether it be in poetry, in prose, or in art, before which the voice of criticism is dumb—the art that speaks straight to the soul of the world. Few of us can hope to achieve that, and I think perhaps if I were to choose any words with which to conclude, I would choose those that may be taken either for your work or for ours—the words that Browning put into the mouth of Andrea del Sarto, "I, painting from myself and to myself, know what I do, am unmoved by men's blame or their praise either." (Cheers.)

CHAPTER VII

SOCIAL TOASTS

THE LADIES

Hints.—This toast is usually proposed by the youngest bachelor in the company, and it is best to address it to both ladies and gentlemen, not as we have heard at least once, to the gentlemen only. Some speakers give the impression in their speeches of a patronizing feeling towards women: they like them as a body but they feel superior themselves. This is, of course, the height of bad form and must be avoided. The toast should be frank, laudatory, and whole-hearted. If it does not come naturally and easy to a speaker to say well of the ladies, he had better leave the toast to someone else. A little humour helps to make a success.

SPECIMEN

Ladies and Gentlemen,—This ought, I believe, to be one of the easiest of all toasts to propose, but, personally, I find it very difficult. There are so many things I want to say and could say if I were able to unravel my thoughts, but, being just a mere man, they crowd into my mind so that I do not know where to begin.

I do not want to be accused of trying to gild unrefined gold, but, frankly, how can I say in a few moments all the nice things it is possible to utter about women? Of course it is an impossibility. Men are all right in their way, but if we are ill or in need of sympathy, if we want comforting, I know I would rather have the care, the sympathy, and the comfort of a woman than a man—than fifty men even. Life, in our young days, would have been a very cheerless sort of existence had it not been for our mothers and sisters, and, I understand, the same can be said of wives in later life. I am not very good at quoting but I think it was Thomas Otway who said :

"O woman, lovely woman nature made thee
To temper man ; we had been brutes without you."

To my mind he strikes the right note. Think of a colony of men living without the refining influence of women! How terribly rough and uncouth we males would become.

Of course, I know a great deal of nonsense is talked about women. George R. Sims once wrote :

"Lor'! but women's rum cattle to deal with
The first man found that to his cost,
And I reckon it's just through a woman,
The last man on earth'll be lost."

Now, I don't believe he would have dared to say any such thing about them had he believed what he said to be true. He would have been afraid. No, he was trading on their generosity.

But do not let me go rambling on. Gentlemen, I ask you to fill your glasses to the very brim and to drink heartily—"The Ladies."

USEFUL QUOTATIONS

I for one venerate a petticoat.—*Byron.*

The sea, the fire and women are the three evils.

Even honey in excess becomes gall.

Angels listen when she speaks.

Her tea she sweetens, as she sips, with scandal.

The female woman is one of the greatest institutions of which this land can boast.—*Artemus Ward.*

She raised a mortal to the skies,
He drew an angel down!—*Dryden.*

Great women belong to history and to self-sacrifice.—
Leigh Hunt.

The most beautiful object in the world, it will be allowed, is a beautiful woman.—*Macaulay.*

Women forgive injuries, but never forget slights.—
Sam Slick.

Nature was in earnest when she made women.—
O. W. Holmes.

Where women are, the better things are implied if not spoken.—" Table Talk."

A Lady's Reply To The Toast Of The Ladies

Hints.—It is usual for a gentleman to return thanks on behalf of the ladies for this toast; but it is becoming more and more the custom for a lady to do so. Indeed, it is only right that one of the so-called weaker sex should take the matter in hand if there is anyone competent to do so. The company will not expect a great show of oratory from her, as audiences are notoriously considerate to women when they speak. We have heard two or three speeches from women on such occasions, when the opportunity has been grasped of upbraiding men for their attitude towards the female sex. This is taking a rather mean advantage, and, though we hold no views on the matter, it appears to us that this is not an occasion when contentious matters should be brought into a speech.

SPECIMEN

Ladies and Gentlemen,—I have it on good authority that quite a number of gentlemen were anxious to make the reply on behalf of the ladies. But while I take this as a great compliment to our sex, I feel strongly that a woman ought to perform the task; and that is why you see me standing here to-night. We women have claimed the right of standing on our own feet; I think we have already proved abundantly that we can do it. Therefore we must not shield ourselves on such an occasion as this behind the good nature of some gentleman who is willing to perform our proper duties.

A number of inspiring things have been said to-night about women. Now, I want to say one uncharitable thing about men, if you will permit me. It is just this—you men spoil us. Personally, I feel, in my own mind, that if all the affectionate things you say of women are true, it is simply because you make us what we are. A good man makes a good woman and vice versa. Women are extremely responsive and, by treating us well, you have us at your feet. Therefore the nice things you say about us recoil on your own heads and only my modesty prevents me from saying in a plainer way what I mean.

Before concluding, may I thank you heartily on behalf of the ladies here for your genial toast. We appreciate it to the full.

USEFUL QUOTATIONS

Talk to woman about religion, she sighs; talk to her of love, she simpers; talk to her of art, she yawns; talk to her of science, she goes to sleep; but talk to her of dress and she will give you the entire attention of her ears.

"She is a human who dresses, babbles, and undresses."
—*Alphonso of Castille.*

A shrewd confectioner has taught his parrot to say "Pretty creature" to every lady who enters his shop, and his business is rapidly increasing.

A Bachelor's Reply To The Toast Of The Ladies

Hints.—It is well-nigh impossible for a bachelor to attempt to reply to the toast of "The Ladies" without introducing a humorous vein and speaking of his own ignorance on the matter. Let him approach the task from this angle and his speech may be easily acclaimed the best of the evening.

SPECIMEN

Ladies and Gentlemen,—I'm in an awful fix. I have

been called upon to reply to the toast of the ladies and what do I really know about the matter ? I'm a bachelor. I'm sure I have your sympathy—I mean because I'm a bachelor, not because I'm in a fix. Well, I suppose I can only blame myself ; but I can see one way out of the matter, and that is to lead some blushing bride to the altar before there is time for me to be called upon again to reply to such a toast. Ah, I notice a very old friend who has pricked up his ears at that remark. Let me tell him that this is neither the time nor the place to divulge bosom secrets.

But I am getting away from the point. *Revenons à nos moutons,* as the French people are supposed to say. I sincerely believe all the nice things that the proposer of the toast uttered about the ladies. As, however, the only real knowledge I have about them has been gleaned from the funny papers, I think I may be allowed to ask a few questions. Do wives in real life drive their husbands into the bankruptcy courts with millinery bills ? Is it true that if the tin-opener gets lost the wife cannot prepare her husband's dinner ? Was there ever a wife who wanted to make some sponge-trifle and so repaired to the nearest chemist in order to procure the sponge ? I pause for a reply.

Ladies and gentlemen, I'm fooling. (Pause.) I had a mother—she was a ministering angel. My sister, God bless her ! And I know other women. Yes. They change light into darkness and the world without them would be no fit place for man. All the things that have been said of them, charming though they were, fall short of the mark.

As far as a man can, I thank you most cordially on behalf of the ladies.

USEFUL QUOTATIONS

Girl graduates wear gowns precisely like those worn by men graduates. The only way to tell the difference is to wait for a mouse.

The only time when a woman prefers to be alone is when a line full of washing comes down in the mud.

Oh ! woman, fairest flower of earth,
  Since first our race began,
Oh ! be our love, our angel still.
  Don't try to be a man !—*E. W. Cole.*

I have always thought that every woman should marry, and no man.—*Disraeli.*

NOTE.—Will women ever return the compliment and introduce the toast of *The Men* ? This piquant point in banquet etiquette is raised by Sir Kenneth D. Mackenzie, Bart., in the " Express." It has a special interest at the moment when so many " all women " dinners are taking place.

The writer says, " The toast of *The Ladies* is one which always meets with acclamation when proposed at a gathering of men with women present, or when they are unable to be, as at messes. Now that women have so many clubs and associations of their own, and are linked together in so many interests and activities, I often wonder whether one day they will return the compliment at some dinner they are giving, and propose *The Men*. Let us hope the toast won't be *The Gentlemen*."

The writer goes on to suggest that as the toast of *The Ladies* is usually proposed by a bachelor, the new toast of *The Men* ought to be voiced by a young, unmarried lady. But will it be " proper " ? Would it not involve an implication that an unmarried lady might possibly resent ? In any case, the matter is full of interest and all we can do is to await developments.

TOAST TO THE BRIDE AND BRIDEGROOM

Hints.—If ever a speech should be brief it is this one.

Time is needed for more important diversions, but the "health" must be proposed, and it should be said in as few words as can be neatly contrived. It is necessary to remind some speakers that the married couple are probably feeling their position and that unpleasant allusions add considerably to their embarrassment and should be omitted.

SPECIMEN

Ladies and Gentlemen,—The making of speeches is an art of which I have little experience. But I feel impelled to call your attention to a little ceremony which I think we ought not to omit. Before we speed them on their journey, we must drink a bumper toast to the happy pair who have to-day embarked upon a great adventure. Of late we have heard much in regard to the matrimonial venture—we have been told that it is going out of fashion, that it is a lottery in which the prizes are all blanks, and much more to the same effect; but I am inclined to think that the explanation of these vapourings is that they emanate from the bridegroom's unsuccessful rivals! For there is no doubt in my mind that he has secured a prize, and that she, in her turn, has by no means drawn a blank. They agree with me, you see—observe it in their faces!

Hitherto I have been a contented bachelor; but I must confess that to-day I envy my old friend the visions that I know he sees; and I cannot say more than that I wish from the bottom of my heart that all his hopes may be fulfilled, and that he and his sweet bride will live long and happily to prove to me the error of my bachelor ways! Ladies and gentlemen, let us drink to the long life, prosperity, and, above all, the happiness of the Bride and Groom.

USEFUL QUOTATIONS

Every man can rule an ill wife but him that has her.

Every couple is not a pair.

Alas! she married another. They frequently do. I hope she is happy—because I am.—*Artemus Ward.*

One was never married and that's his hell :
Another is and that's his plague.—*Burton.*

My dear, my better half.—*Sir Philip Sidney.*

Reply By The Bridegroom

(Including Toast to Bridesmaids)

Hints.—As a rule the bridegroom's reply is brief; indeed it often consists of no more than a few suitable words of thanks. Nobody expects a flow of oratory from him on this occasion. If he should feel disposed to deliver a regular speech, such as the following, he must go warily. While he can say what a fortunate man he considers himself, he must avoid giving a list of the bride's good qualities; but he can mention how considerately the members of her family have always treated him. The moment is a good one to put such a fact on record. If the wife feels disposed, she may rise and make a remark or two, but as a rule she remains silent or just says, "I thank you all very much," or, "It has been a glorious time and you have all been very kind."

SPECIMEN

Ladies and Gentlemen,—I thank you all for your kind thoughts. With so many warm friends, I fail to see why we should ever lack the happiness you wish us. For whatever may be in store for us, if we are to experience some of the trials and troubles that are mankind's common lot, I am sure that friendship such as yours will enable us to meet them with courage and surmount them with success.

I would like to say that I certainly intend to show my friend Mr. —— the error of his ways. So well do I know his worth, that I recommend him unreservedly to the single ladies present; and so great is my esteem for the fair sex, that I recommend them even more unreservedly to his attention. And by the mutual interest I see already displayed, I am confident that before very long there will be interesting developments! We have only to wait and see! Meanwhile, in thanking you again, on behalf of my wife and myself, for your kindly good wishes, I wish to thank especially the ladies who have supported my wife in her trying ordeal, which, I secretly believe, she has enjoyed thoroughly, aud I beg leave to give you a further toast. Ladies and gentlemen, "To the Bridesmaids." May they all officiate at at least one more wedding!

USEFUL QUOTATIONS

A widow cut out her own daughter in the good graces of her lover and married him herself. To obtain revenge for this most unmotherly trick, the daughter set her cap at the young man's rich father, of whom he was the only heir, and actually married him, and had heirs, to the infinite annoyance of her stepchild.

A workman went to sleep at his bench, and as his head fell forward his hair was caught in the machinery. Before he was really awake, he shouted out, "Let go, wife, you are hurting me."

The first year of marriage is always an adjustment—the rest is the same thing.

Man's best possession is a sympathetic wife.

Thy wife is a constellation of virtues; she's the moon, and thou art the man in the moon.—*Congreve.*

Marriage must be a relation either of sympathy or of conquest.—*George Eliot.*

A nation stands or falls with the sanctity of its domestic ties.—*Robertson.*

The Health of the Bridesmaids

Hints.—This is by no means an easy speech to make, as there is so little real matter to rely on. A few congratulatory remarks must form the basis of the theme, and these coupled with some topical suggestions will help the speaker to complete his short oration.

SPECIMEN

Ladies and Gentlemen,—I have a very pleasant duty to perform, and that is to propose the health of the bridesmaids. On such an occasion as this we are liable to centre our chief thoughts on the bride and bridegroom, but I know these two fortunate people will not begrudge a little of your enthusiasm for the ladies who have acted as bridesmaids. Their work may not appear very arduous but, personally, I think it is, and I am sure you will all agree with me when I say that they have performed the duties very admirably. The bride assures me that Miss A. [the chief bridesmaid] has given her a considerable amount of assistance in selecting and arranging the things for the new home. And I am bold enough to hope that Miss A. will at no distant date have to plan a home of her very own. In fact, my advice to all the bridesmaids is to follow the example of the happy bride at the very first opportunity. I see by your smiles that you all agree fully with my sentiments. That being so, I will conclude my remarks with the " Health of the Bridesmaids."

USEFUL QUOTATIONS

The woman that deliberates is lost.—*Addison.*

All thoughts, all passions, all delights,
  Whatever stirs this mortal frame,
Are all but ministers of Love,
  And feed his sacred flame.—*Coleridge.*

Nature intended that woman should be her masterpiece.
—*Lessing.*

Would you hurt a woman worst, aim at her affections.—
Lew Wallace.

The Best Man Replies To The Toast Of The Bridesmaids

Hints.—The best man must attend very closely to the speech of the one who proposes the toast of the bridesmaids, for it will help him with suggestions for his own speech. Here, again, there is very little real matter to dwell on, and his sheet-anchor will be a few congratulatory remarks coupled with any topical tit-bit which he can glean from the ceremony.

SPECIMEN

Ladies and Gentlemen,—At a wedding nobody takes much notice of the men—the bridegroom excepted, of course. And that being so, I am afraid very few people appreciate how onerous my duties were. The best man has, in my opinion, the hardest task of all, for he has to keep an eye not only on the bridegroom but on all the bridesmaids. I rather appreciated my task, however, because—well, look at the bridesmaids! I read in a fashion book the other day that weddings are being celebrated more and more without bridesmaids. My only hope is that the book was wrong, for what a joy they impart to the proceedings! A bachelor, as I am, is apt at first to feel that nothing is worth while once the bridegroom has carried off his bride; but the bridesmaids do help to revive our interest in women-folk. And it is because of the radiance they shed on the proceedings that I heartily agree with the proposer of the toast. In conclusion, may I say on behalf of the bridesmaids, thank you very much.

USEFUL QUOTATIONS

Of all actions of a man's life, his marriage does least concern other people; yet of all actions of our life 'tis most meddled with by other people.—" Table Talk."

Well-married, a man is winged; ill-matched, he is shackled.—*Beecher.*

The most precious possession that ever comes to a man in this world is a woman's heart.—*Holland.*

A Christening Toast

Hints.—There is no regular form of proposal for this toast, and it is only made when the gathering partakes of a formal character. It is open to anyone present to rise and make the proposal, but on a grandfather of the infant or one of the godfathers the duty chiefly devolves. The speech should be of a happy, cheerful character, and wishes for the infant's future happiness ought to be expressed. A compliment to the mother and father may well be included.

SPECIMEN

(Proposed by a Grandfather)

Ladies and Gentlemen [or " Friends " if the first address is too formal],—I rise to propose the toast of health, happiness, and long life to the little stranger. As the little fellow is not in a position to stand up for himself, I must be careful not to say anything bad about him. But who could say anything but kind words of such a dear little innocent chap ? To-day, he has made his first real appearance in public, and I trust it is the beginning of a successful life in this hard work-a-day world. I am sure, if heredity is anything to go by, that he ought to make his mark. Both his mother and his father can claim more than an ordinary share of perseverence and determination, and, of course, I am his grandfather. But, apart from all joking, I only hope he will grow up to be a strong, upright, fearless man—one who does right for right's sake. If he comforts his mother, in times to come, as much as his mother has comforted me, then all will be well. Friends, the health of the Little Stranger, and may he live long and die happy.

USEFUL QUOTATIONS

Every baby born into the world is a finer one than the last.—*Dickens.*

Children are the last word of human imperfection. They cry, my dear; they put vexatious questions; they demand to be fed, to be washed, to be educated, to have their noses blowed; and when the time comes, they break our hearts, as I break this piece of sugar.—*R. L. S.*

A Birthday Toast

Hints.—The one who proposes this toast must avoid fulsome praise, which will merely strike a note of insincerity. On the other hand, it will be quite in order to point out the good qualities of the one whose birthday is being celebrated. As the proposer is a close friend, he should know some tales worth relating about the person in question, and, if they are at the expense of the proposer, they will be enjoyed all the more.

SPECIMEN

Gentlemen,—For some reason or other several of you have conspired to force on me the duty of proposing the toast of the evening. My natural modesty would prevent me assuming such prominence of my own accord; but since you wish it, and since the duty is one that is in itself a pleasure and an honour, I will endeavour to overcome my diffidence. I despair, however, of doing my subject justice. Of what use is it for me to attempt to enumerate the sterling qualities of him in whose honour this little gathering is held? He is the very old friend of all of us, I think; and for myself, I can say that I value his friendship as my most precious possession. My high opinion of him is shared by all with whom he has come in contact, both in public and in private life—of that I am sure. We have evidence of it in his popularity and prominence in all our local affairs. His generous hospitality is proverbial, and he is an ever-ready friend in need. No words of mine, as I say, can do him justice; and, in any case, his praise is superfluous at a gathering like this. So I will come to the point, and ask you to fill your glasses and drink Mr. ——'s very good health, wishing him "Many happy returns of the day!"

USEFUL QUOTATIONS

The ornament of a house is the friends who frequent it.
—*Emerson.*

A friend may well be reckoned the masterpiece of nature.
—*Emerson.*

If he have not a friend, he may quit the stage.—*Bacon.*

Be slow in choosing a friend, slower in changing.
—*Franklin.*

The highest friendship must always lead us to the highest pleasure.—*Fielding.*

Friendship is the gift of the gods, and the most precious boon to man.—*Disraeli.*

Reply To a Birthday Toast

Hints.—Express surprise about all the good things said of you and do not add to them. Be brief.

SPECIMEN

Gentlemen,—I am afraid Mr. A. is not a very truthful man. He has said a number of kind things about me which hardly spare my blushes. I would that they were all correct; but being a mere ordinary mortal and not one of Bernard Shaw's supermen, I feel that I fall considerably short of the mark. Mr. A. is a good fellow, nevertheless, and when he says all these nice things he does it largely to instil me with a desire to live up to his ideals. Well, I will do my best. I have certainly tried in the past and now I will try harder, for Mr. A. is too stanch a friend to let down. I think I have said all I ought, and now let me thank you all for the way you have received the toast. Gentlemen, thank you.

At a Coming of Age

Hints.—See under the head of " A Birthday Toast."

SPECIMEN

Ladies and Gentlemen,—It is now my pleasant duty to propose the health of the hero of the day. This is a great occasion for him—to-day he enters man's estate ; I think you will all agree with me that he is a worthy addition to our ranks. But I do not intend to make a sententious oration. This is a convivial meeting, and we are here to enjoy ourselves ; and neither you nor I will do that if I continue this very stuttering utterance. My duty is simply to ask you to toast our friend in the good old-fashioned way. So, gentlemen, fill up and drink up to our good friend Mr.——.

" For he's a jolly good fellow ! "

USEFUL QUOTATIONS

The youth of a nation are the trustees of posterity, —*Disraeli.*

They can conquer who believe they can.—*Emerson.*

Hitch your wagon to a star.—*Emerson.*

A wise man makes more opportunities than he finds. —*Bacon.*

If you think you are beaten you are.
  If you think you dare not, you don't.
If you'd like to win, but think you can't,
  It's fifty to one you won't.

To youth I have but three words of counsel,—work, Work, WORK.

If youth be a defect, it is one that we outgrow only too soon.—*Lowell.*

Reply By The Person Who Has Come Of Age

Hints.—Be brief and avoid self-praise. Thank those to whom you are personally indebted.

SPECIMEN

Ladies and Gentlemen,—You have heard the very kind remarks of Mr. A. First, I must thank him right heartily for all he has said. I do not know that all the compliments he has lavished on me are quite correct to the letter. But whether they are or not, he has set before me an ideal which I must endeavour in every way to live up to. Certainly, this occasion has inspired me, and I must keep the memories ever in mind. It is a splendid " send off " into the sphere of manhood. Of course, I am fortunate in the matter of parentage. My father and mother you all esteem, I am sure, and any good qualities I may possess I owe first to them and then to such valued friends as Mr. A. He has given me much encouragement in my business life and I should be ungrateful if I did not record the fact here. I mean to carry on the good tradition of my father ; it will be a hard task I know, but I am going to do my best. In conclusion, let me thank you all right heartily for the way you have received the toast. Ladies and gentlemen, thank you.

USEFUL QUOTATIONS

In general those parents have the most reverence who most deserve it."—*Johnson.*

Labour is the law of happiness.—*Stevens.*

What I do not wish men to do to me, I also wish not to do to them.—*Confucius.*

In the ordinary business of life, industry can do anything which genius can do, and very many things which it cannot. —*Beecher.*

To be ignorant of one's ignorance is the malady of the ignorant.—"Table Talk."

Those who make the worst use of their time most complain of its shortness.—*La Bruyère.*

At a Christmas Dinner

(A Family Gathering)

Hints—The Christmas dinner is, more than any other, the occasion of family gatherings. While toasts and speeches would be out of place in many circles, at others it permits of little displays of affection which could not be introduced otherwise. When in doubt as to whether to make a speech or not, take the bull by the horns and make it. Let it be simple, affectionate, and breathing the spirit which Christmas engenders. The opening address must not be of the "Ladies and gentlemen" order, but something far more friendly. Here we suppose that paterfamilias is delivering the little oration.

SPECIMEN

My dear Children,—I am speaking for Mother as well as myself. It is a joy unspeakable for me to stand at this table and see all your bright faces. Christmas brings us many pleasures, but none are so delightful as the reunion of families. When sons and daughters have grown up and flown away to homes of their own, it is a very difficult matter for them to be brought together; but Christmas comes to our aid and sends out a magic spell which effects the blessed reunion. Bob and Phyllis have come home from boarding-school, Mary has arrived with her husband Frank, Joan has a few days respite from her office, and Donald has a week's leave from his regiment. Moreover, Joan and Phyllis have each brought a school chum whose acquaintances we are right glad to make. So, we are all here under the old roof, chatting and laughing and feasting as befits the occasion.

I cannot tell you how glad Mother was when she received the letters, one by one, announcing the fact that our family circle would be complete on this great day. It is a grand thing for a mother to know that her sons and daughters long to be by her side at Yuletide ; and let me just say that your letters showed that Christmas would not be a real Christmas for you if you did not come home.

While we are rejoicing, do not let us forget the true meaning of Christmas, and let us hope that happiness reigns supreme in countless homes, as it does here.

Fill up your glasses, hold them high, and then drink to the double toast of "The Spirit of Christmas" and your "Mother."

USEFUL QUOTATIONS

Here's a health to all those that we love.
Here's a health to all those that love us.
Here's a health to all those that love them that love those
That love them that love those that love us.

May we kiss those we please, and please those we kiss.

The mother we love and the friend we trust.

Where there is a mother in the house, matters speed well.
—"Table Talk."

At a Christmas Dinner

(A Mixed Gathering of Friends and Family)

Hints.—Much that was said under the previous head applies in this case, but the theme must be based on broader lines. The spirit of Christmas must be dealt with fuller and the question of home-ties more briefly. However, the note should be one of cheer and conviviality.

SPECIMEN

Ladies and Gentlemen,—The old order changeth and giveth place to new, says the poet; but while I welcome progress in most things I sincerely trust that the good old English Christmas will never change as long as the Union Jack flies over the Mother Country. Christmas, as we celebrate it, cannot be improved upon. It is, *par excellence*, the time of festivity and goodwill. It gathers together families and friends, the young and the old, the rich and the poor. Here we rejoice because our little family is once again reunited and because valued friends have honoured us with their presence. It is indeed a grand time. The hardest hearts are softened and even Scrooge could not resist the spirit of goodwill. Christmas is, I say, a grand institution.

> There's a time for joy, and a time for sorrow,
> But one's to-day and the other's to-morrow.

Therefore, ladies and gentlemen, let us make the most of to-day. You perhaps have heard this little verse by Carolyn Wells:

> When the turkey's on the table and the candles on the tree,
> I'm jest about as happy as I ever wanta be.
> My children gathered round me an' my neighbours settin' by,
> I couldn't be no happier, an' I don't wanta try.

That expresses my feelings exactly and my wife, I know, thinks the same.

Ladies and gentlemen, the toast of " Christmas."

USEFUL QUOTATIONS

Let not the useless sorrow
Pursue you night and morrow ;
If e'er you hoped, hope now.
Take heart, uncloud your faces
And join in our embraces
Under the holly bough.—*Mackay.*

Christmas times are full of cheer,
And Christmas comes but once a year.

Christmas comes ! He comes, he comes,
Hollies in the window greet him
Gifts precede him, bells proclaim him,
Every mouth delights to name him.
—*Leigh Hunt.*

On New Year's Night

Hints.—This is an occasion for a few words and a toast, but a long speech is usually out of the question. The chief point to emphasize is success to those present and absent friends in the New Year.

SPECIMEN

Friends,—The bells have just rung out the Old Year and ushered in the New. It is a great moment—a trifle solemn, perhaps—but nevertheless one that causes us to pause and wonder what the coming year has in store for us. May it bring happiness and blessings to us all, individually. There are sure to be moments of doubt and uncertainty, but may the " ups " loom far greater than the " downs," and may we have the fortitude and strength to smile at our adversities. Above all, my sincere hope is that every one of you may be here in exactly a year's time to say, as now, " Success to the New Year."

USEFUL QUOTATIONS

Ring in the valiant man and free,
The larger heart, the kindlier hand;
Ring out the darkness of the land,
Ring in the Christ that is to be.

Here's to the good that survives
The toil and the trust of it all,
And may all the ill of the year we fulfil
Depart with the year that's awa'.

Chapter VIII

SPORTING TOASTS

A Toast to "Our Opponents"

Hints.—The great thing in such a speech as this is to speak of the friendly rivalry that the match has caused. If your own side has won, make little of the success, and dwell on the difficulty your men experienced before they could claim a win for themselves. If you have lost, do not bemoan the absence of your best players or claim that your side was unlucky. Say you lost to a superior team.

SPECIMEN

(Proposed by the captain of one of the teams at a match dinner.)

Gentlemen,—You have greatly honoured me in selecting me to act as your chairman to-night, and I take this early opportunity of discharging what is perhaps the most pleasant of the duties which devolve upon my office—that is, the proposal of a toast to our opponents. The —— team have to-day given us a lesson in the way football should be played; but the game, although it went against us, was, nevertheless, enjoyable—to me, at any rate. I am not, of course, going to bore you with excuses for our failure. We did our best, every man of us; but our adversaries, on this occasion, we must admit, did better. Every member of my team will agree with me that the wonderful defence which we encountered is deserving of the highest compliment. Those sturdy backs, —— and ——, if they will permit me to say so, played a wonderfully skilful, hard, and clean game, and I, for one, shall remember not to underestimate their prowess at our next meeting! At that next meeting of course, our positions will be reversed—I have no doubt of it! I should be guilty of disloyalty if I thought otherwise! But I acknowledge that our task will be no easy one, and I look forward with particular pleasure to what I am sure will be one of the best games of the season. To-day we have enjoyed a great match; after all, victory or defeat matters little to the true lover of the national game. We would sooner lose a hard game, such as to-day's, than win an easy one—you will all agree with that, I know. The play's the thing, gentlemen! No team can expect always to win; but next time you shall see things! Meanwhile, let us do honour where honour is due. Gentlemen, "Our Worthy Opponents."

USEFUL QUOTATIONS

The firmest friendships have been formed in mutual adversity, as iron is most strongly united by the fiercest flame.—*Colton.*

Great men often rejoice at crosses of fortune, just as brave soldiers do in wars.—*Seneca.*

Who misses or wins the prize
  Go lose or conquer as you can;
But if you fall or if you rise,
  Be still, pray God, a gentleman.

Reply To The Toast Of "Our Opponents"

Hints.—As for the preceding toast.

SPECIMEN

Mr. Chairman and Gentlemen,—On behalf of my fellow-players, I rise to thank you most heartily for the high tribute you have paid us; but, Mr. Chairman, I must protest that you have been too complimentary. Our success was gratifying to us, naturally; but we must not forget that Dame Fortune helped us in no little degree. Had she been more impartial with her favours—well, the issue might have been very different.

Personally, I can say that the "wonderful defence" referred to was hard put to it on several occasions this afternoon. If we made a good show, it was because a formidable attack demanded of us our very best. I, in my turn, can assure you that I have resolved to bear well in mind that splendid short-passing combination which worried me more than a little to-day! And there is a left wing which I have privately decided will require special attention at our next meeting!

With all our chairman has said I am in thorough agreement: a fast, hard game is the thing we look for and enjoy, no matter what the result. Football—the playing of it, I mean—brings out all that is best in a man. The selfish individualist has no place in the game; a man must play for his team, and in the doing so he learns self-denial as well as self-reliance. What is more, he learns to respect an honourable opponent, and to accept defeat generously and without loss of confidence, as you have shown us.

In conclusion, gentlemen, I must again thank you for the hearty reception and splendid game you have given us.

USEFUL QUOTATIONS

As for the preceding Toast.

Here's to the memories of the past, the joys of the present, and the hopes of time to come.

May we look forward to better things without belittling the things that are.

TOAST TO BOTH THE TEAMS

Hints.—After a match, it is a frequent arrangement to hold a dinner, at which both the home and visiting teams are present. One plan is to toast the sides separately; another is to bring all the players into one toast. The latter is usually to be preferred as time is thereby saved. Moreover, if the toasts are given separately there is a great inducement for the speakers to draw unfriendly comparisons between the two teams. This toast can be made to apply not only to football or cricket but to almost any sport which is played by teams.

SPECIMEN

Gentlemen,—The business I am now called upon to perform is of a very pleasant character. It is to propose the toast of both teams. Many of you—I might say, most of you—here present witnessed, this afternoon, a splendid match and, really, gentlemen, though one side scored more than the other, I think you will agree with me when I say that there is very little to choose between the two. Both sides played their part according to the best traditions of English sportsmen. I congratulate the winners and my sympathies are offered to the losers. To the latter, I would add that there will be many future occasions, I trust, of meeting the winners, and they must hope for better luck next time. The winners need not look for an easy victory on that occasion; they will have to fight every inch of the way if they are to repeat their success.

Both sides, I must say, are fortunate in their captains, who are men of outstanding talent. And now, I will end my little discourse with the request that you all fill your glasses and raise them high in proclaiming the health of the two teams.

USEFUL QUOTATIONS

Success is sweet: the sweeter if long delayed and attained through manifold struggles and defeats.

—"Table Talk."

The team that never meets a better one never need lose.

Every success needs its consolation.—*Eliot.*

The talent of success is nothing more than doing what you can do well: and doing well whatever you do, without a thought of fame.—*Longfellow.*

At an Anglers' Dinner

Hints.—Anglers are proverbially jolly fellows; they are also saddled with another trait, that of telling tall stories. These characteristics are made use of in almost every speech relating to them, and the person who is preparing such a speech will do well to bear these facts in mind; but he should temper his statements with charity. If the speech is to be of a high class, a good many suggestions may be found in "The Compleat Angler."

SPECIMEN

Comrades of the Rod and Line,—Your chairman has been angling for someone to propose the toast "Success to Angling," and he has hooked me. It is one of the worst catches he has ever made, for I stand before you like a fish out of water. I really don't know what to say, because this is a matter quite out of my line. But anglers are not greatly concerned with speeches; they have learnt that silence is golden and they know how to hold their tongues for hours together. There is no occupation where speech is so little needed. They say that patience is a virtue; if that be so, we who are gathered here together to-night must be very virtuous. We sit for hours, symbols of faith and hope, while charity is what I trust you are going to extend to me for wearying you with this speech. There is one thing that I want to ask: Why is it that whenever a good old country inn is christened after us there is always the adjective "jolly" prefixed to the name? It is always the "Jolly Angler"—never the "Grave Angler," or any other kind of angler. Friends, there must be a reason; as a body, we must be jolly or those who give the names to inns would have found us out.

So, my jolly comrades, fill up your glasses and before I am tempted to tell any tall yarns, so frequently imputed to us, drink deep to the success of angling.

USEFUL QUOTATIONS

An angler was stopping at an inn, situated close to a river which provided good fishing, and, desirous of getting some bait, he said to the servant-maid:

"I say, girl, can I get horse-flies round here?" The girl looked wooden. "Have you never seen a horse-fly in these parts?" he inquired.

"Naa, sir," said the girl, "but I wance seed a coo jump over a gate!"

We may say of angling as Dr. Boteler said of strawberries: "Doubtless God could have made a better berry, but doubtless God never did"; and so, if I might be a judge, God never did make a more calm, quiet, innocent recreation than angling.—*Walton.*

Dinna gut your fish till you get them.

At a Boating Club Dinner

Hints.—Most of the hints given already in this chapter will prove useful under this head.

SPECIMEN

Gentlemen,—We are now coming towards the close of a sporting day and a jolly evening, and my final duty as chairman is to call on you for one last toast, to the success of our Club. Other speakers have spoken of the stirring events of the day—our gains, our losses, and our hopes and intentions in regard to the future. I am afraid, however, that one worthy individual has not received his due meed of praise. I refer to the Clerk of the Weather. Without his kind assistance our regatta could scarcely have been such a dazzling success.

I am afraid that time will not permit me to say all that is in my mind; but, before closing, I would like to add my quota to what the last speaker has said in praise of our worthy host. I have been behind the scenes, and I know that he has strained every effort to make our evening a complete and noteworthy success. His excellent fare and splendid arrangements have, I know, been thoroughly appreciated; but all good things must have an end. Therefore, gentlemen, the last toast, please—and bumpers; "Success to the —— Rowing Club!"

USEFUL QUOTATIONS

A varied selection can be made from previous quotations given in this chapter.

GOLF.—THE HEALTH OF THE GOLD MEDALLIST

Hints.—As this toast is made in favour of the prowess of an individual, it may well be devoted largely to a recital of that person's rise to fame in golf. A brief sketch of his previous successes, coupled with a few words declaiming his sportsmanlike character should be included.

SPECIMEN

(At a Golf Club Dinner)

Mr. Chairman, Ladies, and Gentlemen,—On occasions like this, and in proposing a toast that is necessarily a pleasurable duty, it may be permitted for one to be momentarily autobiographical. I well remember, with somewhat mixed emotions, how, after cooling my heels in a queue at the first tee, I addressed the ball in my first match. I had been favoured in my initial practices with more than the usual luck that falls to the lot of the novice. But at the first tee everything was different. Doubtless many of you have experienced that awful oozing away of the feeling of certitude and self-assurance with which a round is started. I experienced it to the full on that occasion; and the memory of that awful ordeal of frantic attempts to reach the first green will never leave me.

Although since then I have made some little progress in "the royal and ancient game"—which satisfies me more perhaps than the partners who are unfortunate enough to share my rounds—I have, if possible, an even more profound admiration nowadays for the man who plays "straight and long" than I had in the far-off days of my novitiate.

"Lies" in golf are proverbially "hard." But lying is easy. You will not need reminding of this. Your own accounts of a match, of course, never vary in the slightest degree from the cold, bare facts! But your neighbour's account of *his* match is one that you generally feel is handled with a somewhat careless regard for the truth!

When, however, one is hearing the account of a round played by a third person, one is reasonably sure that the performance will not suffer from magnification. And it was my good fortune recently to witness the performance of our good friend ——, when, by his masterful play and wonderful resource in extracting himself from difficulties, he succeeded not only in winning the club's gold medal, but in putting up a record that will always be the admiration of his fellow-members, and an incentive to them to try to follow in his wake. And the impression I received was that it was magic—not golf such as we play!

It is unnecessary for me to refer to the fine sportsmanlike character of our friend—we all know him too well. I feel that I shall have everyone present with me when I express the wish that our guest's form may never be below that of his medal round, and that our best efforts will be devoted to getting individually as near to it as we can. Gentlemen, "The Winner of the Gold Medal!"

USEFUL QUOTATIONS

Gentlemen with broad chests and ambitious intentions do sometimes disappoint their friends by failing to carry the world before them.—*Eliot.*

"I had a round of golf with my wife this morning."

"Which won?" The husband did not answer. "Which won?" asked the friend a second time.

"Which one?" thundered the husband. "How many wives do you think I have? Do you take me for a Turk?"

At a Football Dinner

Hints.—The merits of the game, its universal appeal, and its character-forming qualities are the chief points to make in this speech.

SPECIMEN

Gentlemen,—I rise to propose the toast of "Success to Football." Gentlemen, I look upon Football as the national game, for I make bold to say that no other pastime has so many devotees. From the moment when we first enter upon school-life to the time we have to lay aside strenuous games, football is the favourite of the majority, easily beating cricket, golf, tennis, etc., in its fascinations for the multitude. The war years are not so long ago that many of us have forgotten the joy a few kicks at the ball gave us in our all-too-brief moments of leisure when we were in the back trenches. And, gentlemen, you have all heard that remark about British endurance being born on the playing-fields of Eton. Well, I am prepared to wager that a football was there. More than any other game, football teaches us to give and take; it teaches us to be skilful, smart, and neat; it teaches us the art of losing gracefully. Can as much be said of any other pastime? Gentlemen, I think not. The matches you have played in various parts of the country have brought you in contact with many opposing teams and valuable friendships have been thereby formed. There is thus a social side to this national game the worth of which must not be ignored. Personally, were I to find myself with a friend on a desert island, I would prefer to have a football than almost any other luxury—I would prefer it even to a bag of gold.

In some quarters football is decried as being a pastime for the rougher elements, and, to prove the point, we are reminded of those followers who travel up to London on Cup-Tie Saturday wearing new caps. Gentlemen, could any argument be more absurd? Those rough-looking customers have rough lives to live; their hands are rough, their speech is perhaps rough, but their hearts may be right. If football brightens the lives of such individuals, good luck to football. It is doing a good work. It is keeping men from baser things.

But, gentlemen, enough. You agree with me, I am sure, and all that remains for me to ask is that you drink deeply to the success of the national game—good old football!

USEFUL QUOTATIONS

See under previous heads in this chapter.

Success to Lawn Tennis

Hints.—The occasions on which such a toast as this might be proposed are many and the wording of the speech will have to be regulated accordingly. The great point in preparing the matter is to avoid names, as, by mentioning people, invidious distinctions are immediately drawn. The effect the weather has had on the season's play, the financial position of the club, and future arrangements are safe matters to discuss.

SPECIMEN

Ladies and Gentlemen,—I think I am voicing the opinion of you all when I claim that, thanks to the weather and thanks, also, to our Honorary Secretary, the matches to-day have brought our summer season to a successful close.

In reviewing the activities of the Club, I think we members have much for which to be grateful. Our membership list is growing and what I might call the point of saturation is almost reached. Our finances are such that we are able to send out tenders for the making of half a dozen hard courts. These will, of course, be extremely welcome in the winter months. And our successes have never been so numerous. It is this latter fact that I view with most pleasure. Nearly every match we have played with friendly rival teams has proved a victory for us. It speaks well for our players, and I think we ought to give them a cheer.

There is no doubt that the royal game of tennis was never so popular as it is to-day. Witness the improvements at Wimbledon and the crowds of folk who now flock there. Witness, also, the private courts that are springing up on all sides in outer Suburbia. There never was such a demand in the shops for rackets and things, and everybody now, from lisping infants to genial greybeards, may be seen improving their game at the net.

Ladies and gentlemen, I must detain you no longer. I will now ask you to support heartily the toast " Success to Lawn Tennis," and I think I may add that this Club wishes to tender its gratitude to the committee for arranging such an enjoyable season.

USEFUL QUOTATIONS

They also serve who also stand and wait.—*Milton.*

CHAPTER IX

POLITICAL SPEECHES

INTRODUCING A CANDIDATE FOR ELECTION

Hints.—In no class of speech is it more necessary to make yourself on good terms with the audience than in political speeches. When proposing a convivial toast the guests will meet you in a friendly spirit, but in politics there is always a certain element only too ready to find fault with your remarks. Therefore, be on the safe side and, in the present case, say nothing controversial; leave that to the prospective candidate. Point out the good qualities of your man, try to be sincere, and ask for a good hearing for him.

SPECIMEN

Ladies and Gentlemen,—My first and chief duty as chairman this evening is to introduce to you Mr. —— as a candidate to represent the interests of this Borough in Parliament. A great many of you, possibly, know him better than I do. But, although my acquaintance with him has been of short duration, it has been sufficient to convince me that he is in every way an able exponent of the principles of the —— Party, and a man upon whom we may safely rely for the furtherance of the Party's aims. His election address should by this time have come into the hands of every elector in the Borough, and its straightforward and explicit nature will, I think, go a long way towards securing his success in the coming contest. As this meeting has been convened mainly to afford you the opportunity of hearing from Mr. —— himself his opinions upon the pressing questions of the day, I will trespass upon your time no more than is necessary to request you earnestly to give him a fair and patient hearing. Any questions you may desire to put he will be only too pleased to answer at the conclusion of his address. For my own part, I am satisfied that his address will be well worth your attention; and I may add that he already has the promise of my support and vote. Ladies and gentlemen, Mr. —— will now address you.

Proposing a Candidate for a Municipal Election

Mr. Chairman, Ladies and Gentlemen,—It is with great pleasure and some pride that I rise to propose my friend Mr. —— as candidate for election to the —— Town Council. Those of you who know him as well as I do will have no hesitation in agreeing with me that he is the man we want. For the past few weeks he has been doing everything humanly possible to bring before his fellow-townsmen the principles and programme for which he stands. He is peculiarly adapted, in my opinion, to secure for the town, if he is elected, the consideration of those matters which have been, for reasons it is not my place to mention, so long neglected. Our Local Authority needs young men of energy and thoroughness more at the present time than ever before. It is impossible to disguise the fact that matters in this town are in a bad state—that is, as far as the interest of the workers, who are the bulk of the electors, is concerned. I would remind you of the . . . These improvements, for which we have so long looked in vain, will never be secured without considerable pressure. The particular reforms most immediately desirable and attainable have been, and will be again, indicated by Mr. —— himself; but I would emphasize to you this point, that however much we agree that they are desirable, we shall never obtain them unless we return as councillors men of definite purpose and perseverance. I unhesitatingly say that, from his past record, we know Mr. —— to be such a man; and I therefore strongly recommend the electors to give him their undivided support.

USEFUL QUOTATIONS

He serves his party best, who serves the country best.
—*Hayes.*

There is no perfecter endowment in man than political virtue.—*Plutarch.*

Wait and see.—*Asquith.*

Supporting the Proposed Adoption of a Political Candidate

Hints.—*As under* the previous head.

SPECIMEN

Mr. Chairman, Ladies, and Gentlemen,—After hearing Mr. ——'s able exposition of his views, and, moreover, by reason of a knowledge of his character—gained during a long and intimate acquaintance—I have no hesitation in supporting the proposition that Mr. —— be adopted as the —— Party candidate to contest the coming election. For the benefit of those who, perhaps, are unacquainted with Mr. ——, I would like to give a brief account of the excellent work which he has done locally in connexion with the —— and the —— during the last five years. The —— Organization, to which he is now acting as general secretary, owes, I think I may say, practically the whole of its strength and efficiency to his untiring efforts, etc. . . . Those with whom Mr. —— comes in daily contact are unanimous in the opinion that his personality and energy are of inestimable value to any interests which it is his intention to further. That he has the interests of the electors of this Division at heart, I think should be plain to all; and that he intends to devote his whole attention to the matters of which he has just spoken is my firm conviction. As a citizen, Mr. —— is universally esteemed; and as a politician he has shown us that he possesses common sense coupled with fine ideals and worthy aspirations. Ladies and gentlemen, I have very great pleasure in supporting the proposal that we adopt Mr. —— as our candidate.

USEFUL QUOTATIONS

In the present case these are hardly advisable, but *see under* previous head.

Speech by the Proposed Candidate

Hints.—The speech should be a careful summary of your political aims, omitting, however, those that may not be palatable to your audience. If an election address has been drawn up, or is in preparation, your first speech and the address should coincide in views. You must be extremely careful to avoid offending people who can help you by support. Some have extremely peculiar views although of your shade of politics. Get to know from your immediate followers of any such opinions and try to avoid all mention of them. With your hecklers endeavour to be affable or genial at first—such a line of action may disarm them. But if they persist, be firm but do not lose your temper. To do so is fatal.

SPECIMEN

It is almost useless to provide a specimen speech, as what you say should reflect the statements of your election address. Plan the speech so that it amplifies and explains the address and finish by offering to answer questions.

USEFUL QUOTATIONS

Pride is at the bottom of all great mistakes.

All our wants, beyond those which a very moderate income will supply, are purely imaginary.

Liars and cowards, they are the same thing.

Work is the great cure of all maladies and miseries that ever beset mankind.—*Carlyle.*

The proud will sooner lose their way than ask.

A halter made of silk is a halter still.—*Cibber.*

He that is willing to work finds it hard to wait.

Idle bodies are generally busybodies.

Every ass loves to hear himself bray.

Can anybody remember when times were not hard and money not scarce ?—*Emerson.*

Annual income £20 ; annual expenditure £19 19s. 6d. Result, happiness. Annual income £20 ; annual expenditure £20 ought and six. Result, misery.—*Mr. Micawber.*

We cannot eat the fruit while the tree is in blossom.
—*Disraeli.*

A thing done right to-day means less trouble to-morrow.

Education isn't all in leading a horse to water; it is also in giving him a taste for it.

There's a dignity in labour.—*Swain.*

Opposing the Recommendation of a Candidate for Election

Hints.—This is not a particularly happy speech to have to make, but, if your convictions deem it necessary, undertake the unpleasant duty fearlessly. First of all, be careful not to utter a libel. Avoid as much as possible saying Mr. A. is so-and-so or has done such-and-such a thing, if it is derogatory. Say, rather, "In my opinion, Mr. A. is so-and-so. . . ." A libel is then much less likely to be committed, and your statement is just as damaging to his cause. As you must have some good reasons for opposing the candidature, state them clearly and in proper order. Express your regrets that you feel bound to put your opinions on record and make some sort of apology for being a dissenter.

SPECIMEN

Mr. Chairman, Ladies, and Gentlemen,—I have listened to Mr. ——'s address with considerable interest, and I am willing to pay him the tribute that he has stated his opinions honestly and well. You, Mr. Chairman, have advanced to us several good reasons demonstrating his suitability to represent us. Nevertheless, I feel it my duty to put before this meeting several points to which I think we should give further consideration before adopting him as our candidate. In the first place, Mr. ——, although he has touched upon the subject, has not dealt thoroughly with the question of . . . His replies to various questions on the matter have been, to say the least, somewhat meagre. I will not say they were evasive; but I suggest to you that this question of . . . is of vital importance to us as electors, and is not one which can be satisfactorily dealt with by a policy such as Mr. —— has adopted in referring to it. He has expressed a general sort of agreement with what he terms "the Party's views" on the subject. To me it seems obvious that he has not devoted serious attention to it, and I protest that since the question is one that bulks large in our programme our duty is to select and elect for this constituency a candidate who thoroughly understands this matter, and who, moreover, intends to use his first and strongest efforts towards the furtherance of our aims in regard to it.

In regard to one or two other points, namely, . . . and . . . , it also appears that Mr. ——'s attitude is hardly representative of our own. We have at previous meetings passed resolutions strongly in favour of . . . . In regard to this, I respectfully suggest to you again that Mr. —— does not seem to take up a very definite position; and what little he has said on the matter does not appear to me to be in entire agreement with our own opinions. I maintain, Mr. Chairman, that we need a candidate with very definite knowledge and intentions in regard to these matters; Mr. —— will, I am sure, understand that what I say is said in no spirit of malice. But I honestly feel that much further consideration is necessary before we come to our final decision.

USEFUL QUOTATIONS

He was always for ill, and never for good.—*Scott.*

I may not be Meethosalem but I am not a child in arms.
—*Little Dorrit.*

His discourse sounds big but means nothing.

Better not do the deed than weep it done.—*Prior.*

Go with the times and not blow against the winds.

I hate the philosopher who is not wise for himself. —*Euripides.*

As headstrong as an "allegory" on the banks of the Nile.—*Sheridan.*

Truth alone wounds.

Good rarely came from good advice.—*Byron.*

Advice is seldom welcome: and those who want it the most, always like it the least.—*Earl of Chesterfield.*

CHAPTER X

BUSINESS SPEECHES

THE CHAIRMAN'S SPEECH AT THE ANNUAL MEETING OF A COMPANY

Hints.—A speech such as this must take one of many forms, according to the measure of the success of the year's trading. It must, of course, be a résumé of the past year as far as the company is concerned. The following " specimen " will indicate to the new hand how he should set out his remarks.

SPECIMEN

Gentlemen,—I take it that it is the will of the meeting that the report and accounts which have been printed and sent out to you individually shall be taken as read. I will assume in the absence of dissent that you agree to this.

It is my duty now on behalf of the Board to move, " That the directors' report and the accounts for the year ended —— be received and adopted." I do not think any material good can come from a minute examination of the figures, seeing that you have had them in your hands for some two or three weeks, but it may be advisable to make some broad comments regarding them.

When you come to consider the balance-sheet, I think the results of the past year's trading must give the shareholders very substantial cause for congratulation. It seems to me a very sound balance-sheet, showing that our business is progressing in a satisfactory way. [Here give reasons, i.e. debenture holders paid off, liabilities reduced, depreciation and reserve account strengthened, etc.]

You will have noticed from the report that at the end of the year we had a profit of £—— at our disposal. Out of this the Preference dividend appropriates £——, which leaves £——. This sum will provide a dividend of £—— on the Ordinary shares and leave £—— to be carried forward.

[Here give a résumé of the past year's history relating to buildings, plant, new outlets for business, staff, etc.]

At this point it is my privilege to give you some forecast of what, in my opinion, will be the result of next year's trading. I always disclaim any prophetic capability, but, as far as I can judge, the coming year should be even more successful than the last. [Reasons.]

Finally, I have to say that according to the memorandum of the Company, Mr. A. retires from the Board of Directors and offers himself for re-election.

That, gentlemen, subject to any questions which you may wish to ask me, is all I have to say regarding the state of your Company, which I consider is in a flourishing condition.

[At this point, someone must rise and second the motion which is, "That the Directors' Report and the Accounts for the year ended —— be received and adopted." Next, the chairman will reply to questions, and, lastly, a vote on the motion is taken. This is usually done by a show of hands.]

USEFUL QUOTATIONS

These are almost unnecessary, as the speech should be of a severely practical character. However, if such are required, a good selection will be found in Chapter XII.

A Ratepayers' Meeting

(By the Chairman)

Hints.—In this case a few words of thanks are necessary at the outset, if it is the first speech made by the chairman after election. These may well be followed by some mention of the present-day enlightenment of voters; and then the business in hand is reached. Be affable throughout, endeavour to give a good impression, and, if you are at all inclined to be nervous, try to think of the business and not yourself.

SPECIMEN

Ladies and Gentlemen,—I feel you have done me a great honour in making me your chairman, and I know you will excuse me if I say I am very proud. It is not only a post carrying with it a certain dignity but a good many arduous duties. I can assure you that these I will endeavour to fulfil not only to the best of my ability but to your complete satisfaction.

Time was when the ratepayers paid their rates after duly grumbling, and did no more; but those days are past, and, if I may say so, those who pay the piper now call the tune, as they certainly should. I am quite certain that you will watch our movements from the public gallery, and I sincerely hope that it will be always full to overflowing. Nothing will keep us up to the mark like a full gallery of keen observers. Those of you who cannot attend will be able to follow our operations by reading the reports in the local paper. And let me say this: we are here to serve you and to do your will. Unless we know your wishes we cannot put them into force. Therefore, let us know your wants. You can write to us, you can write to the local papers, you can do many things in this way. But do not be apathetic; do not sit down and wait for us to guess what you want. As long as you make yourselves heard (please, do not be too hard on us if we do not get everything done your way in a fortnight) things will right themselves as speedily as they should.

I should like to compliment you on your choice of councillors. Excluding myself, I can assure you that they are an able body of men. Never were they more fitted to attend to the business of the locality. Of course, the millennium has not been reached, but we must be patient.

And I am sure you will be glad to know that our first item of business is to reopen the old question, which has been shelved for years, of providing a swimming bath and wash-houses. No one knows more on this subject and is better fitted to speak on it than Mr. A., and I have great pleasure in calling upon him to propose the first resolution.

USEFUL QUOTATIONS

Going fast is no advantage unless you go in the right direction.

Wisdom is knowing what to do next. Skill is knowing how to do it. Virtue is doing it.

Laws like houses lean on one another.—*Burke.*

A worthy man is not mindful of past injuries.

Water, air, and cleanliness are the chief articles in my pharmacopœia.

Smiles and good health are close relations. The smiling face bespeaks health of mind and body and freedom from those little ills which, often enough, underlie and create the frowns which come from nowhere.

Great haste makes great waste.

Trade Union Secretary's Report of the Year's Work

Hints.—The following specimen will, with slight alterations of subject-matter, serve for any case that may arise. Great powers of eloquence are not required in such a speech—merely a clear way of setting out the facts.

SPECIMEN

Mr. Chairman and Gentlemen,—In making this report of the things we have accomplished in our third year, I feel that, despite undoubted failures in one or two directions, our achievements have been such that we can afford to be proud of the year's work as a whole. Perhaps the most satisfactory information I have to impart is that our membership has increased from —— at the beginning of the year to —— at the present time. We may also congratulate ourselves on the result of our efforts in regard to . . . . At the outset things looked extremely black for us in that matter; but, thanks to the energy and perseverance of Mr. —— and Mr. ——, after negotiations extending over a period of four months, a definite and fairly satisfactory settlement was reached. In the matter of . . . which I know is uppermost in your minds at present, a conclusion has not yet been reached; but I think that I may say that so far our prospects in that direction may be considered good. Our other activities I will go over briefly in order that you may obtain a comprehensive view of the progress we have made.

We have held —— meetings, at which the attendances have, on the whole, steadily increased.

Of social gatherings we have held in all ——: they have been increasingly popular, and have proved on the whole profitable.

We have also . . . , etc.

The general state of our finances you will have seen by the copies of the balance-sheet which have been circulated; but there are one or two items therein about which I wish to say a few words in explanation. The expenditure on . . . was necessitated by . . . ., etc.

In conclusion, gentlemen, I would point out that, although we have made gratifying progress, much still remains to be done. In the year that is now before us we must not relax effort—rather, we must increase it—if we are fully to justify ourselves and the principles by which we stand.

USEFUL QUOTATIONS

(Such are seldom required)

There's no good thing in all the world got without labour at the back of it.—*Eden Phillpotts.*

Wealth be a very tricky addition to life. It's a temptation to the strong to taste power, and a lure to the weak to seek pleasure. A trial that both too often sink under.

It is a sad thing when men have neither wit to speak well nor judgment to hold their tongues.—*La Bruyère.*

Intemperance in talk makes a dreadful havoc in the heart.—*Wilson.*

The true use of speech is not so much to express our wants as to conceal them.—*Goldsmith.*

Speech by an Official of a Trade Union Submitting a Question to a General Meeting

Hints.—Eloquence is not needed, but a knowledge of the facts is. State your case on the lines suggested below; be sure that your reasoning is sound; and when you have made out your points stop.

SPECIMEN

Mr. Chairman and Comrades,—This meeting has been called in order that careful consideration may be given to the question of the desirability or otherwise of . . . The question is one of peculiar difficulty; it not only involves considerations of finance and organization, it involves questions of policy and tactics, and—what is more important—the political views held by the individual members of our organization. In our membership we have men of all shades of political opinion—Conservatives, Liberals, and Labour. Many hold their particular political views very strongly; so that in considering this matter, no sort of general agreement can be hoped for unless some criterion is applied which represents a point of view tenable by every member whatever his political conviction. The Committee have directed me to suggest to you that the criterion we should apply to a question of this kind is a very simple one—namely, whether, considered in the light of an investment, the project is one which is likely to yield a good return for the time, money, and energy which we should have to put into it. Our organization exists mainly for the purpose of securing for its members better conditions. Will the project of . . . help us in that object to a degree commensurate with its cost? That is the question which I urge that each of you should put to himself.

I will now briefly set out the various arguments for and against the project. The case against is as follows:

First, . . . second, . . ., etc. The case in favour is as follows: First, . . .; second, . . ., etc.

In conclusion, the Committee wish me to say that they are themselves led by these latter considerations to recommend the proposal as one which it will pay us to adopt.

USEFUL QUOTATIONS

See under previous head.

Cricket Club Secretary's Report

Hints.—The following specimen may, with slight alteration of subject-matter, be used by the secretary of any sports club, whether football, tennis, croquet, etc., in making his annual report. Oratory is unnecessary—the facts are the thing. A little humour is permissible.

SPECIMEN

Mr. Chairman and Gentlemen—In preparing this report to place before you, I have endeavoured to be as brief as possible, and to arrange it in such a way that members—new members particularly—may obtain a comprehensive view of the club's development during the past year.

First, as to last season. Matches played numbered ——, of which we won ——, drew ——, and lost ——. On —— occasions visiting teams were entertained to lunch and tea. It was decided at last year's General Meeting to make this a rule, and I think it has received general approbation, and rendered the club popular.

Our membership during the year has increased very considerably—from —— to ——. This is very gratifying, and I attribute it mainly to our having obtained the new club-house and ground. There are some financial details in connexion with the matter with which the treasurer will deal later.

With regard to the acquisition of the new club ground, I would remind you that the project was embarked upon not without considerable opposition, on grounds of finance and expediency, from a proportion of our old members. Inquiries as to alternative accommodation were accordingly made; but the Committee's final decision was the right one, I think—for our present quarters are convenient and spacious, and have resulted, as I say, in raising considerably the status and popularity of the club.

Some new nets were acquired also toward the end of last season, were very well patronized, and will undoubtedly be required this season.

I must also refer to the three social events we held during the winter. They were each extremely successful, and I have been pressed by many members for a greater number in the future.

Coming now to my own work—the preliminaries for the

coming season—I must first inform you that it has been decided to run two elevens. Matches to the number of —— for the first eleven, and —— for the second eleven are already arranged; and "home" and "away" events have been fitted in so that the teams will have the use of our own ground alternately.

Finally, I wish to mention that many members have written urging the formation of a tennis club. I am inclined to favour the idea, since we have ample room for two or three courts; and I will be glad to undertake the arrangements if the project meets with general approval.

USEFUL QUOTATIONS

The English winter—ending in July to recommence in August.—*Byron.*

The Eleven—may they always be steady in adversity and upright beside the *wicked.*

Bat and ball. Long may they be honestly opposed in the field.

Chapter XI

MISCELLANEOUS TOASTS AND SPEECHES

Toast of " The Visitors " at a Firm's Annual Outing

Hints.—This toast is appreciated most when proposed by the head of the firm. The speech must vary with the type of visitor. Where these are educated people, there would be no harm in quoting, say, from one of the poets ; but a passage from Dryden or Milton would fall on very deaf ears if the firm's workmen were of a rough type. The latter would enjoy two or three well-told jokes mingled with complimentary remarks regarding the loyalty of the staff.

SPECIMEN

(By the Head of the Firm)

Ladies and Gentlemen, Friends,—It is a great pleasure to me to be amongst you again on the occasion of the annual outing. And I feel very proud that so many wives and sweethearts have accepted the firm's invitation to honour us with their company. After all is said and done, earning one's living is not one of the most exciting ways of passing the time, but I do believe that in our factory and office we are as contented a band of workers as could be found anywhere. A good many " bosses " think of everything in terms of pounds, shillings, and pence, but at the old works we claim that a loyal staff is worth more than mere cash. Ladies and gentlemen, we are fortunate in having that loyal staff, and you are valued members of that staff. I do not want to go into details of the last balance-sheet, but you have all probably heard whispers about it being a good one. Well, let me say that luck and loyalty make a good balance-sheet; leave out either ingredient and your year's work becomes a failure.

Now, let me beg of you to make the most of this festive occasion. I don't want to put it quite as forcibly as Phil May's coster, who said to his wife, "I've brought yer out ter enjoy yerself and you've jolly well got ter." Nevertheless, let me exhort you all to enjoy yourselves to the full, so that when you reach home you will be dead beat. To-morrow is Sunday, so you will not have to be up early. I hope it will keep fine throughout the day, but an English summer is a very fickle thing and there are some doubtful looking clouds coming up. You know the old joke about our summers, I suppose. An American was complaining about them. "You can never tell when you Britishers are going to have a summer," he said. "Why, last year it was on a Friday and the year before on a Monday." Well, I hope it will be to-day this year, don't you? I must now ask you, friends, to raise your glasses high and drink deeply to our visitors.

USEFUL QUOTATIONS

Work is the grand cure for all the maladies and miseries that ever beset mankind—honest work.—*Carlyle.*

Man's record upon this wild world is the record of work, and of work alone.—*Holland.*

No man has a right to be idle if he can get work to do, even if he be as rich as Crœsus.—*Holland.*

REPLY TO THE TOAST OF "THE VISITORS"

Hints.—Though a visitor may reply to the toast, it is more likely that a worker of the firm will undertake the task. He should thank the head of the firm for his kind words and make some allusion to the good feeling which exists between the staff and the owners. Probably, he will wish, also, to make some remarks on the weather, whatever it happens to be.

SPECIMEN

Ladies and Gentlemen,—You have all heard the kind words uttered by our respected head. Those words are typical of the gentleman who spoke them. They flow from his tongue not only on high-days and holidays, such as the day we are now enjoying, but when the hurry and bustle of factory life make most men anything but genial. I have been, I hope, a useful worker in the factory for nigh on twenty years, and during all that time I have received nothing but kindness and, I believe, respect from him and his partners. And, I know I am not alone in my praises. In fact, all the hands who don't mind work will say exactly the same. Of course, it is quite open to me to stand here and say a number of things that are not borne out by fact; but there is no necessity. We have a Head who will listen to reason, and, moreover, does listen to reason, even when it is against his interests. No wonder that so many of us have grown old in his service!

But, ladies and gentlemen, I won't detain you much longer. We not only admire the man who has provided this day of feasting and festival for us, but we appreciate the fact that he has spared the time to come and be with us. It is a joy for him to be here, and if he finds the occasion as pleasant as we find it, then he is experiencing a jolly good day. I know you all thank him for his kindness and if ever there was a jolly good fellow it is our "Boss."

USEFUL QUOTATIONS

Work, according to my feeling, is as necessary as eating and sleeping.—*Humboldt.*

We have a certain work to do for our bread, and that is to be done strenuously; other work for our delight, and that is to be done heartily; neither is to be done by halves or shifts.—*Ruskin.*

In all the world there is nothing so remarkable as a great man, nothing so rare, nothing so well repays study.—*Parker.*

The greatest truths are the simplest; and so are the greatest men.—*Hare.*

The gifts of genius are far greater than the givers themselves venture to suppose.—*Harvey.*

Many men have been capable of doing a wise thing, many more a cunning thing, but very few a generous thing.
—*Pope.*

Toast of "The Firm" at the Annual Dinner

Hints.—This toast will usually be proposed by an employee. He should think out some facts which reflect credit on the heads of the firm and weave the speech around them. Although a little exaggeration of the good qualities of the "leaders" is permissible, this should not be overdone. Any remark which is insincere is likely to recoil, sooner or later, on the one who utters it.

SPECIMEN

Mr. Chairman, Ladies (if any present), and Gentlemen.—For some reason, not quite understood by me, I have been asked to propose the toast of "The Firm." This is an honour and a pleasure which I gladly accept. For twenty years I have been a member of the staff. Let me add they have been twenty years of happiness. I am not going to say that the work is light or that it is easy. Often it is just the contrary. But when you know that if you do your best all will be well, then hard work and difficult work can be cheerfully undertaken. Looking around the room I see a number of friends, nodding in assent of my remarks. Those friends know, as I do, that the directorate is composed of gentlemen who are the very essence of kindness and consideration. We are, indeed, a fortunate band of workers, for, ladies and gentlemen, it is not every staff in the city that has such a model body of "heads." It is a well-known fact that when a man or woman is fortunate enough to become attached to our staff he or she endeavours to remain on it, and the inducements to fly off elsewhere practically do not exist. Perhaps, I should not say it, but I rather think that some of the success of our firm is due to the fact that we should not like to slack off when our "heads" treat us so well. Of course, most of the success is the result of careful organization at the top. But, ladies and gentlemen, I do not wish to appear fulsome. May I now ask you to raise your glasses and join with me in drinking to the success of the Firm and the health of the Directorate?

USEFUL QUOTATIONS

You cannot make the poor man rich by making the rich man poor.

The progress of the world has not come by pulling men down. It has come by building them up.

From a bad crow, a bad egg.

Evil gains are equivalent to losses.

He is a fool who leaves certainties for uncertainties.

Corporations have no souls.—*Thurlow*.

A true man hates no one.

'Tis want of courage not to be content.

Smiles are the sunshine of our sunless days. Through fog, through mist, between the falling rain drops, they light a cheery way.

Reply By The Head Of The Firm

Hints.—The reply should consist of three main features—(1) A partial refutation of the generous remarks of the proposer, (2) thanks for the sentiments expressed, and (3) a hope that the future will be as prosperous as the past. At such gatherings, the opportunity is often taken of hinting at fresh developments that the directorate has in mind.

SPECIMEN

Ladies (if any present) and Gentlemen,—You all heard the cordial expressions of Mr. A. when he proposed my health. Well, I am rather wondering if he was pulling my leg, for he said such a lot of charming things which I know I don't deserve. However, I do believe that our staff is a contented body. I should be terribly upset if it were not. It is my desire and that of my colleagues, the other directors, that all who work for us should find life congenial in our service. To wish otherwise would not only be inhuman—it would be folly in our own interests. The days when a clerk suffers the conditions of a Bob Cratchit are past and ought to be; and service should not only be adequately paid for but it should be honoured.

Many firms, such as ours, suffer a great deal from industrial unrest, which must mean a financial loss to them. We, on the other hand, do not know what such unrest is—we have never experienced it. Why? Well, simply because you are men and women above such tactics. We share a portion of our profits with you—I am alluding to the scheme of bonusses—and you know full well that our success is yours.

I'm now going to take you into my confidence. The past year's trading has been a splendid success and the directors are thinking of increasing their premises and launching out in one or two new directions. There will be a number of new posts created and many fresh positions of trust.

I am afraid I have already occupied too much precious time in making rambling statements, so I will now conclude by saying that I thank you all for these new expressions of confidence. Ladies and gentlemen, thank you.

USEFUL QUOTATIONS

If limiting output will help the working man, China ought to be a working man's paradise.

A man who works and saves is a capitalist.

The road to hell is paved with good intentions.

Little is done when everybody is master.

He who seeketh trouble never misseth it.

Let us all be happy and live within our means, even if we have to borrow the money to do it.—*Artemus Ward.*

Self-trust is the first secret of success.—*Emerson.*

The man who makes no mistakes does not usually make anything.

Toast To "The Press"

Hints.—Very often the speaker commences by putting on record some slightly caustic remarks about the Press, merely for fun, and then retracts in his concluding sentences. There is no harm in such a course in the case of an able speaker; but for those of less experience we recommend a speech such as the following:

SPECIMEN

Mr. Chairman and Gentlemen.—Of late the Press has been the recipient of much criticism of a sort far removed from kindly. Street-corner orators are for ever denouncing us for taking our opinions direct from newspapers, and are for ever accusing the "Fourth Estate" for furthering the evil designs of some tyrant or other. I suppose that a paper must have its policy—and I do not propose to raise any controversy on such an occasion as this. But it occurs to me that as "a nation gets the Government it deserves" so does it get the Press that it deserves. In my humble opinion, the chief concern of an editor or newspaper proprietor is to sell his paper, and with that end in view it seems to me that of necessity he supplies the public with what it wants. Granting that our Press has its faults, and is not, for excellent reasons, quite so free and outspoken as some of us would like, at least we must admit that it compares extremely favourably with that of other countries. The Press of this country considering, all things, is an institution of which we may be proud. To all who quarrel with it I would say that its improvement rests with themselves. It cannot be denied that the Press is a really useful factor in the daily life and in the education of the nation. I maintain that the Press of England is at least as good as, if not better than, we deserve, and I call upon you to drink to it, and to Mr. ——, who is, I believe, its representative here to-night.

USEFUL QUOTATIONS

Four hostile newspapers are to be feared more than a thousand bayonets.—*Napoleon.*

Lions are not frightened by cats.

With just enough learning to misquote.—*Byron.*

Amicably if they can, violently if they must.
—*De Quincey.*

It is much easier to be critical than correct.—*Disraeli.*

Newspapers are the schoolmasters of the common people.—*Beecher.*

In these times we fight for ideas, and newspapers are our fortresses.—*Heine.*

Newspapers always excite curiosity. No one ever lays one down without a feeling of disappointment.—*Lamb.*

Reply To The Toast Of "The Press"

Hints.—This should be undertaken by a journalist. The reply will have to depend almost entirely on the subject-matter of the proposal.

SPECIMEN

Mr. Chairman and Gentlemen,—As a Pressman I am used to having showered upon my head recriminations of the nature referred to by Mr. ——. I had intended to say something in defence, but Mr. —— has said it for me. I can, from my professional capacity, bear witness to the truth of his remarks. I can assure you that an editor's sole endeavour is to provide the public with what it wants—that is, as far as is possible. Speaking personally, and on behalf of my brethren of the pen, I may say that in *our* opinion this country has a Press a great deal better than it deserves! These things are bound to be largely a matter of opinion; but from the very kind sentiments that have just been expressed, I am convinced that our efforts are not by any means unappreciated; and I beg of you to accept from me, in the absence of a fitter representative, the assurance that the Press reciprocates your goodwill most heartily.

USEFUL QUOTATIONS

See under previous head.

The Health Of The Bishop

(By a Layman)

Hints.—Such a toast as this may be used on a variety of occasions, and, with slight alteration, may be made to apply to a number of different clerical officials. The main theme is, of course, to point out the unselfish duties and burdens which the clergy, as a body, is ever ready to shoulder. The notoriously small stipends which many clerics receive may be pointed out on some occasions, say when money affairs are being discussed, but it would prove a jarring note to mention the matter at such social gatherings as garden-parties or when the occasion was of a festive character.

SPECIMEN

Gentlemen,—I have been asked, as a layman who interests himself in the welfare of the Church, to propose the health of the Bishop [or other dignitary.] I can assure you all, though you need no assurance, that I undertake this duty with sincere pleasure. You all know the Bishop—that he is a busy man, full of loyalty and sincerity—but I doubt if many here present have any adequate conception of the burdens which he shoulders. Some people clamour for an eight-hour working day. I rather think the Bishop would be looking round for something to do in his spare time if he were given an eight-hour day. I have found him at work at six in the morning and I know he often burns the midnight oil. Gentlemen, it is for us that he labours so unremittingly and we must be, and, I believe, are, correspondingly grateful.

In these days of mercenary feelings it is a very frequent thing to find the Church falling into disfavour with certain types of thought. But our Bishop is a man out of a thousand who has always been able to steer his flock through seas of trouble to havens of tranquillity. For all these good offices we must indeed be grateful. Regarding what I may term his social labours, his work among the sick and needy, I could tell you much that would touch your hearts, but the Bishop is a man who wishes to hide his light under a bushel and I ought not to disregard his feelings.

Gentlemen, I have great pleasure in proposing the health of the Bishop.

USEFUL QUOTATIONS

An honest man's the noblest work of God.—*Pope.*

God often visits us, but most of the while we are not at home.—*Roux.*

To yield reverence to another, to hold ourselves and our

lives at his disposal is the noblest state in which a man can live in this world.—*Ruskin.*

It is well said, in every sense, that a man's religion is the chief fact with regard to him.—*Carlyle.*

Reply To The Health Of The Bishop

(By the Bishop)

Hints.—The chief heads under which this speech should be arranged are (1) An expression of thanks, (2) a mild protest that the toast is too generous in its expressions, (3) the valuable assistance afforded by laymen, (4) a hope that the bond of friendship between the clergy and the congregation will continue, and (5) business matters of special interest at the moment.

SPECIMEN

Gentlemen,—I have to thank you right heartily for the way you have received the toast proposed by Mr. A. It was extremely kind of him to express such generous and genial thoughts. But he has set me thinking rather deeply, because I do not feel that I am entitled to all the splendid things he said about me. It is true we clergy as a body work, and work hard; but it is our duty and we perform such duties cheerfully. I may add that it would be well-nigh impossible for us to perform our task with any measure of success were it not for the loyal support we receive from our lay friends. Mr. A., for instance, is a most valuable helper, ready at all times to give us advice and assistance. As long as the bond of union between the clergy and congregation is as firmly cemented as it is now, all will be well with the spiritual needs of this diocese [parish]. Gentlemen, I thank you most heartily for the way you have accepted the toast.

USEFUL QUOTATIONS

In religion, as in friendship, they who profess most are the least sincere.—*Sheridan.*

Religion is civilization, the highest.—*Disraeli.*

Whatever makes men good Christians makes them good citizens.—*Webster.*

He whose goodness is part of himself is what is called a real man.—*Mencius.*

I would rather have the affectionate regard of my fellow-men than I would have heaps and mines of gold.—*Dickens.*

The future is purchased by the present.—*Johnson.*

A true and noble friendship shrinks not at the greatest of trials.—*Jeremy Taylor.*

When men are friends, there is no need of justice; but when they are just, they still need friendship.—*Aristotle.*

Just praise is only a debt.—*Johnson.*

The Health of the Churchwardens

(By a Minister)

Hints.—By slight alteration this speech may be made to apply to any layman who renders particular assistance to the church officials, whether he be a churchwarden or not. The following specimen should have added to it such details as apply to the person or persons individually.

SPECIMEN

Gentlemen,—It is my special privilege to-night to rise and propose to you the health of the churchwardens. I am rather afraid that many of you here present know very little of these loyal gentlemen. Their work, though arduous, is of a silent, unassuming character and it claims very little attention outside what might be called the inner ring of the Church.

Churchwardens have performed much of the secular

business of Church affairs ever since the early days of Christianity, and the particular gentlemen whom we are honouring to-night are worthy descendants of those we read of in the Bible. They meet me twice a week throughout the year to discuss business matters, but never a week goes by but I have to consult them at odd times on questions which arise without previous warning. They are always most anxious to advise and help me, and, no matter whether it is eight in the morning or eleven at night when I ring the bell of their door, I am welcomed in and given whatever help or information I require.

Gentlemen, I cannot over-estimate the value of their services, and you who have the welfare of your parish at heart must agree with me that we are all deeply indebted to our little body of churchwardens. Our obligation to them is great, and I call upon you to respond in the heartiest manner possible to the toast of "The Churchwardens."

USEFUL QUOTATIONS

You can only make others better by being good yourself.—*Hawers.*

We can all be angry with our neighbour. What we want is to be shown, not his defects, of which we are too conscious, but his merits, to which we are too blind.—*R. L. S.*

A modest man never talks of himself.

Some men deserve praise for what they have done, and others for what they have not done.

There can hardly, I believe, be imagined a more desirable pleasure than that of praise unmixed with any possibility of flattery.—*Sir Richard Steele.*

The Ten Commandments do not need to be re-written so much as re-read.

Reply To The Health Of The Churchwardens

(By a Churchwarden)

Hints.—This reply must be governed largely by what was said by the proposer of the toast. In a general way, however, the subject matter will consist of a disavowal of the kind things uttered by the previous speaker, a short summary of the duties undertaken, and an expression of pleasure that such duties are appreciated. There is no reason why a certain amount of apt humour should not be introduced.

SPECIMEN

Gentlemen,—You have all heard what our Vicar has just told you regarding me and my colleagues. Perhaps you look upon the Vicar as a truthful man. I'm sorry to have to disabuse your minds. He is not a truthful man, and I can prove it. Only last week he told me the following little story. " Story " is, I am afraid, the correct word to use. He was going to Worcester and, when the train reached Banbury, he put his head out of the window and asked a boy pushing a refreshment pram for a Banbury cake. The boy said he had none but would run off an get one. The Vicar gave the boy sixpence and told him to get two, one for himself and the other the boy could eat. In a few moments the youngster came hurrying back with his mouth crammed full with a portion of a cake. " Sorry, mister," said the boy as best he could, considering the disadvantages which a mouthful of bun were sure to cause ; " 'ere's threepence ; they only 'ad one cake left." When he told me that happened to him at Banbury I began to think. Now he has said what he has about me I know. Gentlemen, our Vicar stands condemned as an untruthful man. It is a matter that the churchwardens will have to take up.

But, apart from all joking, I can assure you that the relations which exist between him and us are of a most cordial character. We have to thrash out all sorts of matters and he is ever ready to help us, down to the most minute of details. Our work, instead of being tedious, is a pleasure, and we are indeed fortunate in being led by such an upright man. To say that he is an asset to the parish is to put the case mildly. He is a giant in our midst.

Gentlemen, there are other matters which require your attention to-night and I will detain you no longer; but, in conclusion, I must thank you for the way you have received the toast and I am more than grateful to the Vicar for his splendid eulogy.

USEFUL QUOTATIONS

SUNDAY SCHOOL TEACHER: Can any little boy tell me what children go to Heaven?

NASTY LITTLE BOY: Dead 'uns.

CURATE (slumming, to dirty little urchin): Well, my little man, is your father in work?

LITTLE BOY: Yus.

CURATE: And how long has he been in work?

LITTLE BOY: Two months.

CURATE: What is he doing?

LITTLE BOY: Three months.

The new vicar officiated for the first time, and as the congregation filed out of the church at the end of the service one of the members whispered to a sidesman:

"I have nothing but praise for our new vicar."

"Yes, I know," said the sidesman, "I noticed that when I took the bag along your pew."

VICAR (to local spendthrift): My dear man, you ought not to spend all your week's money.

LOCAL SPENDTHRIFT: I never do, mister. I gets three pounds a week and out of that I only spends two pound ten.

VICAR: Good, my man, and what do you do with the remainder? You bank it, I trust.

SPENDTHRIFT: Oh, no, guv'nor. I gives the rest to the missus. 'Ow d'yer think she'd run the 'ouse else?

PRESENTATION SPEECH ON THE OCCASION OF A RETIRING EMPLOYEE

Hints.—In the present case it is supposed that the employee is retiring on reaching the age-limit. With a very little alteration it can be made to serve where an employee is leaving because of a breakdown in health or to fill a better post. The speech must, of course, be eulogistic, but this is very often overdone, when the remarks lose their value.

SPECIMEN

Ladies and Gentlemen,—My feelings are of a mixed character. We are met here to say "good-bye" to an old friend. Mr. A. is leaving us after twenty-five years of devoted service. I do not like partings, but in this particular case it will prove a great blow, and I am sure that every one of you who has worked with Mr. A. will agree with me.

It is not altogether an easy matter for me to tell you, in a few words, what I think of Mr. A., and, indeed, it will be hardly right and proper that I should—"Good wines need no bush." But it would be ungrateful if I did not remind you of his devotion to his work and his unfailing courtesy to those who were under him. In all the years that I have known him I can honestly say that I have never seen him out of temper. I think that is something for him to be proud of. I am sure that nobody will be able to say that of me when I retire.

In some respects Mr. A. is a very lucky man. He will not have to jump out of bed, swallow down his breakfast, and strap-hang in the train on the way up to the office any more. All his time will be his own, and I sincerely trust that it will be enjoyable—every hour of it. I would like to remind him that, though his old place in the office will be filled by someone else, no one is going to fill his place at our little social functions. I therefore hope he will not forget us, but will turn up to the concerts, whist-drives, sports meetings and so on. I want him to promise on his word of honour that he will.

And now, ladies and gentlemen, I am going to ask him, on your behalf, to accept this little gift. It carries with it our joy at having worked with so fine a gentleman and a wish that he may live long and he happy in his retirement. Ladies and gentlemen, the health of Mr. A.

USEFUL QUOTATIONS

Do all the good you can,
By all the means you can,
In all the ways you can,
In all the places you can,
At all the times you can,
To all the people you can,
As long as ever you can.—*John Wesley.*

The way of a great man is threefold : virtuous, he is free from anxieties ; wise, he is free from perplexities ; bold, he is free from fear.—*Confucius.*

Reply By The Retiring Employee

Hints.—The presentation speech must in a measure govern the reply ; but a simple expression of thanks is often more dignified than a long apologia.

SPECIMEN

Mr. Chairman, Ladies, and Gentlemen,—There is a Japanese proverb which says that " In the hum of the market there is money, but under the cherry tree there is rest." Well, in my garden there is a cherry tree, and it is in my garden that I intend to find rest. You kindly said, Mr. Chairman, that my departure gave you mixed feelings. It is no case of mixed feelings with me. They are all regrets—regrets that my span of useful life has run its course, regrets that greater heights were not climbed, regrets that your genial companionship in the office has come to an end, and so on. It will be a great blow to be severed from the firm in whose service I have grown up. Your kindly expressions are greatly appreciated and your charming gift I shall prize as long as I live. Mr. Chairman, ladies, and gentlemen, may I thank you for all you have said and done, now and in the past. As to my word of honour regarding your social functions, I give it gladly.

USEFUL QUOTATIONS

God did not make men perfect. He made them pilgrims after perfection.—*H. W. Beecher*.

Lost, yesterday, somewhere between sunrise and sunset, two golden hours, each set with sixty diamond minutes. No reward offered, for they are gone for ever.

—*Horace Mann*.

When all is done and said,
  In the end thus shall you find,
He most of all doth bathe in bliss
  That hath a quiet mind.—*Lord Vaux*.

SUCCESS TO THE POLICE FORCE

Hints.—It occasionally occurs that at a dinner of local interests the Police Force is toasted. As a rule, the person making the speech is a member of the municipal council who is not in any way connected with the force. The best way to treat the matter is to endeavour to be mildly humorous, but, of course, the serious side must be touched upon

SPECIMEN

Mr. Chairman, Gentlemen,—It is my pleasant duty to propose the toast "Success to the Police Force." I am afraid that only those of us who are law-abiding citizens can honestly take part in this toast, and all here present who may belong to the Raffles fraternity I would ask to remain seated when we stand to do honour to our gentlemen in blue. I do not know why, but the police have always figured largely in our jokes and in our national humour. I think it must be because, as a body, they are endowed with an unlimited supply of good nature. This is, of course, a great asset to them in the trying work they have to perform. I have only seen one policeman in all my life who lost his temper, and that was in Cologne. If I were asked how the Force could be improved I do not think I could offer a single useful suggestion. It is as near to perfection as things go in this imperfect world.

For policemen, individually, I have a very great affection, and I do not blame cooks and parlourmaids who show little weaknesses on their behalf. That is, if they really do. But do they? We have a cook; but I have never known one of these worthy gentlemen to make a hurried exit from the kitchen on the approach of my wife. I wish they would come and show a special interest in our house: it would add to our feeling of security.

But do not let us think of these gentlemen as mere suppressors of Bill Sykes & Co. Think of their multifarious duties! In regulating traffic they are marvellous. Only the other day I saw a young constable throw himself at the head of a runaway horse. He was a peace-time hero. And have you have ever had a lump in your throat when you have seen a six-foot Robert leading a weeping, lost infant to the station to await some distracted mother? I have, and I am not ashamed to admit it.

I could say much more, in my rambling way, regarding

my affections for these preservers of the peace, but I will desist. In drinking to the toast of the Police Force, let us associate the names of Inspector A. and Station-Sergeants C. and D. They are worthy heads of a worthy body of men.

USEFUL QUOTATIONS

When constabulary's duty to be done, a policeman's lot is not a happy one.—*Gilbert.*

COUNTRY DOCTOR (to his chauffeur): It doesn't matter a hang what speed we go, Charles. I have the village constable in bed with rheumatics.

SUCCESS TO THE FIRE BRIGADE

Hints.—Our remarks concerning the Police Force apply, more or less, in the present case, though the humorous element should be less in evidence and more should be made of the heroic part of a fireman's duties.

SPECIMEN

Mr. Chairman, Gentlemen,—I have never had a fire in my life—I mean, of course, a conflagration necessitating the help of the Brigade; but because I have been fortunate, do not think that I don't put a high value on its usefulness. We should look upon the Fire Brigade as a form of insurance. It is there, ready to come to our aid, even if we don't require it. Of all the money spent in this borough none, I think, should be begrudged less than that which goes to support the Brigade.

Personally, I should make a poor fireman, for I haven't the courage. It must take an enormous amount of pluck to dash into a burning building; but this is what the men may be called upon to do at any minute.

Our Brigade has attained a high standard of efficiency,

and this is due not only to the splendid zeal of the men but to the organization of its Chief, whom we are pleased to have in our midst here to-night. Quite recently, [such and such] improvements have been effected, and these are largely due to his skill and interest in our safety. Therefore, Mr. Chairman, and gentlemen, I have the greatest pleasure in asking you to accord your support, right heartily, to the "Success of the Fire Brigade," and to couple with it the name of Mr. A.

USEFUL QUOTATIONS

Fire—the most tangible of all visible mysteries.
—*Leigh Hunt.*

Forewarned, forearmed: to be prepared is half the victory.—*Cervantes.*

By nothing do men show their character more than by the things they laugh at.—*Goethe.*

Vote of Thanks to a Temperance Lecturer

Hints.—It would be unwise to give a lecture on temperance unless you have gone deeply into the subject, seeing that there are so many points which a troublesome audience might put to vex you. Also, skilled temperance lecturers are to be had quite freely by applying to any of the temperance societies. They will probably do the work better than you. What may very likely come your way is the privilege of proposing a vote of thanks to a temperance lecturer who has spoken to an audience in which you are interested. The following specimen will then be of assistance.

SPECIMEN

Ladies and Gentlemen,—You have all listened to the address of Mr. A. with, I am sure, a good deal of interest. He has put the case for temperance in a very illuminating and, I may say, a very forceful way. Had we any doubts on the matter before to-night I think those doubts must have vanished entirely. The drink evil is a very real evil. Its influence on health is alarming; but, to my mind, worse than the effect it has on the one who drinks it is the effect it has on the home and on the children in the home. A man who drinks to excess spends money that should rightly go in purchasing food and other necessities for his wife and children. His evil habits deprive them of many of the things they have a right to expect. This is a fact that is unanswerable. It is a most glaring instance of the sins of the father being visited upon his children.

Ladies and gentlemen, I have never heard of a man being uplifted by drink; but no one can deny that there are thousands every day who are being degraded by drink. This alone should be a sufficient testimony in favour of temperance.

Our friend Mr. A. has pointed out the effects of alcohol on the body. I would like to add that its so-called stimulating effect is always followed by a feeling of relapse. A glass of whisky will make you, first, lively and then sleepy; it will make you feel, first, warm and, then cold; it will brace you up first, and then let you down. Valuable qualities, you see.

The only good that can be said about alcohol is that, in extremely rare instances, it has kept a person from dying. As a set-off against this, it kills tens of thousands annually.

Ladies and gentlemen, I will not try to add further to Mr. A.'s admirable lecture, but will conclude by proposing a very hearty vote of thanks to him.

USEFUL QUOTATIONS

Alcohol—liquid madness sold at 10d. the quartern.
—*Carlyle.*

Alcohol—the devil in solution.

If abstinence on the part of a temperate drinker would reclaim any drunkard, a man of ordinary humanity would practise it as far as considerations of enjoyment were concerned.—*Lord Bramwell.*

A Chairman's Opening Remarks at a Smoking Concert

Hints.—See Chapter IV.

SPECIMEN

Gentlemen,—I am glad that my official position as chairman this evening does not carry with it very onerous duties. I notice these little functions of ours are growing in popularity, and I judge that their popularity is due to the excellence of the entertainment provided. At any rate, I am quite certain that it is not to hear a verbose chairman that you come; so I will be brief. We have a long and varied programme before us—music, vocal, and instrumental, and a morsel of dramatic art—for all of which we are indebted to Mr. —— and Mr. ——, in whose hands have been all the arrangements. I must remind you of our custom in regard to choruses, and—without offence, I hope—drop you the hint to order your refreshments *between* the items. That is all I need say, I think. We are "all assembled, so let the revels commence." I call upon Mr. —— for the opening item on our programme, which is . . .

USEFUL QUOTATIONS

The range of suitable quotations is in this case unlimited, and the reader is advised to refer to Chapter XII.

An Empire Day Speech

Hints.—Empire Day speeches are required for a variety of audiences from club members to school children. The main theme in all cases must be "patriotism for the Motherland and her far-flung Empire." The following speech may be used for any emergency and any particular colony by slight alteration. The opening address must, of course, be made to suit the audience.

SPECIMEN

Gentlemen,—Events of recent years have brought us who live in the Old Country into close touch with our Colonies. The comradeship of the trenches opened for us a new understanding with our brethren overseas, and established a mutual respect which will bind the British Empire into lasting solidarity. Those heroic achievements in Gallipoli, which have made the word Anzac a synonym for fearlessness, the awful struggles on the Western Front, where the Australian troops showed themselves more than a match for the most highly trained professional soldiers, have demonstrated that the dauntless spirit of the old-time pioneers still persists in their descendants. For the men who went in the early days to make their homes in those far countries were, without doubt, the pick of our manhood—adventurous, hardy, supremely self-reliant, and with that rare courage which is required to face the unknown. They formed a stock from which we can rightly expect great men and great things. The great men we have seen—not in isolated instances, but in battalions; the great things we may see, if we wish, by observing the wonderful advance in commerce and legislation which this young country has made in the space of a few generations. Agricultural and mineral wealth has been developed so that there is scarce a single nation in the old world which does not depend for its support in a large degree upon Australia. The wise laws Australian statesmen have framed go far to prevent the evils which in this country at present cause so much unrest. To any young Britisher with a will to work hard Australia offers a free training, a good start, all reasonable assistance in hard times. Her legislators know that for the development of their country they must have men—of the right sort; and to get those men they are not niggardly in their offers. Australians who are present will bear with me if I seem to dwell overlong upon these matters; it is because I have been impressed by the workmanlike manner in which their country is grappling with present problems and preparing for the future. If Australia but continues as she has begun, I feel inspired to prophesy for her people a great and glorious future. Gentlemen, I give you "The Commonwealth of Australia—may it ever prosper!"

USEFUL QUOTATIONS AND FACTS

The Empire on which the sun never sets.

The All-Red route.

I find the Englishman to be him of all men who stands firmest in his shoes.

What is the best government? That which teaches us to govern ourselves.

Prosperity: and may it ever be the rising sun of our Empire.

The Empire: may the land of our nativity be ever the abode of freedom and the birthplace of heroes.

The Empire is safe, if true within itself.

Be the Empire what it will: with all its faults, it is my Empire still.

The peoples of the Empire are the most enthusiastic in the world. There are others more excitable, but there are none so enthusiastic.

The nation that has no enemies has no following.

The training which makes men happiest in themselves also makes them most serviceable to others.

The British Empire embraces an area of 13,900,000 square miles. The whole world consists of 55,500,000 square miles. Thus about a quarter of the world is British.

The population of the Empire is four hundred and fifty million people. This is slightly more than a fifth of the world's total.

Sixty million British people belong to the white races.

The Empire may be said to have come into being in the year 1583, when Newfoundland became the first colony.

Outside the British Isles, Calcutta is the largest city in the Empire, and Sydney comes second.

Canada was discovered by Cabot in 1497; but not until 1763 did it become a British possession. It was formed into a Dominion in 1867.

Australia was first visited by William Dampier in 1688, but no progress in colonization was made until Captain Cook landed on the East coast in 1770. The Commonwealth was formed in 1900.

The Cape of Good Hope was discovered by Bartholomew Diaz in 1488, while Vasco de Gama landed at Natal in 1497. The Cape was ceded to Britain in 1814. The Union of South Africa was formed in 1909.

Empire Day is May 24th.

Chapter XII

FURTHER USEFUL QUOTATIONS

AN apt quotation is often the means of transforming an otherwise commonplace speech into one of brilliancy. As this is so, we have suggested a variety of such quotations on many of the previous pages. Here we conclude with a miscellaneous selection of not only wise sayings but of lesser-known jokes.

Toasts

Merry met and merry part,
I drink to thee with all my heart.

Hounds stout, horses healthy,
Earths well stopped and foxes plenty.

May we please those we kiss and kiss those we please.

The single married and the married happy.

Sweethearts and wives.

Love to one, friendship to some, and goodwill to all.

Now good digestion wait on appetite: And health on both.—*Shakespeare.*

May we always have a friend and a dinner to give him.

May our friends never be one too few, nor our enemies one too many.

May we never feel want, nor want feeling.

The best of money—matrimony.

Put fire in your work or put your work on the fire.

The sportsman who never beats about the bush.

No woman should marry a teetotaller or a man who does not smoke.—*R. L. S.*

If there were no bad people there would be no good lawyers.—*Dickens.*

There is moderation even in success.—*Disraeli.*

It is a melancholy truth that even great men have their poor relations.—*Dickens.*

He, dying, bequeathed to his son a good name.

A wound, though cured, yet leaves behind a scar

Strange to say what delight we married people have to see these poor fools decoyed into our condition.

—*Samuel Pepys.*

Business goes where it is solicited and stays where it is well treated.

A machine can do most any work a man can do nowadays, but a machine can never think.

It is necessary to entice the buyer to unsaleable wares; good merchandise easily finds a buyer, even though it be hidden away.—*Plautus.*

Sweet is the remembrance of troubles when you are in safety.—*Euripides.*

The belongings of friends are common.—*Pythagoras.*

It is better to be the best of a bad family than to be well born the worst of one's race.

It is better to reign in Hell than serve in Heaven.

When the candle is taken away every woman is alike.

The wise man alone is free and every fool a slave.

Friends are not so easily made as kept.

No speech ever uttered or utterable is worth comparison with silence.—*Carlyle.*

'Tis want of courage not to be content.—*Chesterfield.*

With the persuasive language of a tear.—*Chesterfield.*

I do not hate him near as much as I fear I ought.—*Carlyle.*

He had only one vanity: he thought he could give advice better than any other person.—*Mark Twain.*

He that thinks amiss, concludes worse.

Little boats must keep the shore.

A lady of a "certain age," which means certainly agèd.
—*Byron.*

Pleasure's a sin and sometimes sin's a pleasure.

You know who the critics are? The men who have failed in literature and art.—*Disraeli.*

Danger for danger's sake is senseless.—*Leigh Hunt.*

Young men think old men fools, and old men know young men to be so.—*Metcalf.*

No fools are so troublesome as those who have some wit.
—*La Rochefoucauld.*

It needs brains to be a real fool.

There is no duty we so much underrate as the duty of being happy.

By being happy we bestow anonymous benefits upon the world, which remain unknown even to ourselves, or, when they are disclosed, surprise nobody so much as the benefactor. A happy man or woman is a better thing to find than a Five-pound Note, he is a radiating focus of goodwill.—*R. L. Stevenson.*

Party politics leave me cold. But the countryside of England and the literature of Europe make me glow.
—*George Wyndham.*

Self-reverence self-knowledge, self-control.

These three alone lead life to sovereign power.
—*Tennyson*

He that will not reason is a bigot; he that cannot reason is a fool; he that dare not reason is a slave.
—*Drummond.*

The God to whom little boys say their prayers has a face very like their mother's!—*J. M. Barrie.*

Always play fair, and think fair; and if you win don't crow about it; and if you lose don't fret.—*Eden Phillpotts.*

It is true we are creatures of circumstances, but circumstances are also, in a great measure, the creatures of us.
—*Lord Lytton.*

If someone would give to the Boy Scout movement the price of one Dreadnought we could go near to making Dreadnoughts no longer necessary.—*Robert Baden-Powell.*

That best portion of a good man's life,
His little, nameless, unremembered acts
Of kindness and of love.—*Wordsworth.*

If you want to go into battle, have an Englishman at your right hand, and another at your left, and two immediately in front and two close behind. There is something in the English which seems to guarantee security. Never forget that, even when you are most irritated by the antics of these engaging madmen.—*Voltaire.*

Remember what Simonides said—that he never repented that he had held his tongue, but often that he had spoken.
—*Plutarch.*

I would not give much for that man's Christianity whose dog did not benefit by it.—*Rowland Hill.*

At a banquet: "Well, did they like your speech after the dinner?"

"Rather! When I sat down, everybody said it was the best thing I'd ever done."

"I'm jolly sorry for Eve."

"Why?"

"Well, she never really knew how fashionably she was attired."

"I can see you are a married man, now."

"How?"

"'Cause you have no buttons off your coat and——"

"Yes, that's the first thing my wife did—taught me how to sew them on."

CURATE: So you really think you would have run through all your money had it not been for your wife?

YOUNG BLOOD: Sure of it.

CURATE: And, my good man, how did she stop you spending it all?

YOUNG BLOOD: She spent it first.

IMPECUNIOUS ONE: I would like to settle that little debt of mine.

THE MAN WHO LENT THE MONEY: I'm very glad to hear it; just step into the office.

IMPECUNIOUS ONE: I said I would *like* to; but I can't.

PATIENT: I say, doctor, don't you think it would be a good idea if I packed up and went to a place where the climate was warmer?

DOCTOR: Good Lord! isn't that the very thing I have been trying to prevent?

A clergyman had cause to reprove one of his parishioners. The parishioner lost his temper and, as a parting shot, roared out:

"If I had an imbecile son I would put him to the Church."

"Your father thought differently," replied the cleric meekly.

JUDGE: The prisoner is sentenced to a fine of one hundred dollars and seven days' imprisonment.

PRISONER: Judge, I wish you could reverse your sentence.

JUDGE: Very good then; seven dollars fine and a hundred years' imprisonment.

Apropos of counsel browbeating witnesses in murder trials, the case is recalled where the lawyer looked quizzically at the doctor who was testifying, and said:

"Doctors sometimes make mistakes, don't they?"

"Just as lawyers do, sometimes," was the reply.

"But doctors' mistakes are buried six feet under ground," said the lawyer.

"Yes," said the doctor, "and lawyers' mistakes sometimes swing six feet in the air."

Jones was a fellow with few scruples. There being a new curate in the parish, Jones went up to him in the road and, with a straight face, asked him if he could tell him when was the devil's birthday. The curate gazed on his questioner for a second, and then said :

" Sir, I don't know, but surely you can find out by referring to your family records."

A discussion was once held by the authorities of a certain town as to whether the cemetery adjacent should be surrounded by a wall. Nearly all the members of the Board having expressed their views on the subject, the chairman suggested that a certain silent member, Farmer Jones, should give them the benefit of his valuable judgment ; whereupon that worthy arose and remarked that he did not see the necessity for having a wall at all, for those who were already inside would not in any case escape, while those who were still outside would have no anxiety to get in.

The motorist was a reckless fellow but generous, nevertheless, and he swerved and ran over a fowl which darted across the road. An old woman who lived in a cottage hard by was on the scene immediately. Her face was stern, her features hard and forbidding. Before she could utter a word, the motorist plunged a hand in his pocket and tendered her a Bradbury.

" Here, my good woman," he said apologetically, " this will square matters,"

The sour face softened. " It's good of you," she said ; " now I shall be able to start keeping fowls myself."

SERGEANT BULLY : Now, you blighter, do your bloomin' bootlace up at once.

RECRUIT (married and absent-minded) : All right, darling.

" Weren't you upset when the bank went smash ? "

" No, I only lost my balance."

War Profiteer's Wife: Then you agree to sing at my little party for ten guineas.

Soprano: Yes, ten guineas.

W.P.'s Wife: And you quite understand that I do not wish you to mix with the guests.

Soprano: In that case my fee is five guineas.

Departing Traveller (to the boy in buttons): Run upstairs, boy, as quick as lightning, and see if my umbrella is in room 502. I think I left it in the corner by the wash-stand.

Boy in Buttons (some minutes later): Quite right, sir, it's exactly where you said it was.

Mrs. Quickrich's little party was in full swing, and the French gentleman-visitor had just obliged by giving an admirable rendering of the national anthem of his native land.

"Very jolly toon, sir, and nice action too," said Mrs. Quickrich; "but what I could never hunderstand was why they calls it the Mayonnaise."

"So all your daughters are married now."

"Yes, the last one left us last week."

"It must be nice to get them all off your hands."

"Well, it's nice enough to get your daughters off your hands; but what we don't like is having to keep our sons-in-law on their feet."

"How did you get on at the police court yesterday?"

"Fine."

Mac and Sandy kept two adjoining shops, and one day Mac had a most elegant sun-blind fitted. Sandy admired the blind and said he wished he could afford one like it. A little while later Sandy had a sun-blind put up even better than Mac's. Mac was rather nettled and went in to see Sandy about it.

"Thought you couldn't afford a blind like mine, Sandy, and here you are with a far better one," said Mac.

"Nor could I afford it," retorted Sandy, with a grin. "My customers presented it to me."

"Your customers! How do you mean?"

"Well, it was like this. I put a collection box on the counter and wrote on it *For the Blind.*"

HUSBAND: But why in the name of heaven did you want to insure my life with that canvasser chap? I might live longer than you.

WIFE: Just like you; always looking on the gloomy side of things.

SHE: Did I fill the drawing-room with my voice while I sang that song?

HE: Well, no; you emptied it.

"So you claim that your wife dragged you down to this awful plight?"

"Yes, lidy; she's the cause abs'lutely."

"And how did she ruin you?"

"Well, it's like this. I got 'er three good jobs and she lost 'em all with 'er 'igh-'anded ways."

Recently a soldier was discussing politics in a Paris wineshop with two rubicund workmen.

"Tell us," they asked him, "if one day the down-trodden working-men were to revolt, would you be one to fire on them?"

"I? Never!"

"Bravo! You are a true comrade. Here, master, bring us another bottle; we must stand treat."

The wineshop keeper quickly placed before them the required bottle, and frequent toasts to each other's health ensued. Then one of the workmen put another question to the brave soldier, the friend of the people:

"How many men, brave fellows like yourself, can we count on in the barracks?" he asked.

"All the band; they will act as myself. I play on the big drum, you know," he casually remarked, as he finished the contents of his glass.

The curtain was about to go up when the comedian, who had just proved an utter failure, walked into the manager's office. He flopped into a chair and began to moan.

"What's the matter?" inquired the manager.

"Could you put someone else on in my place?" ejaculated the comedian, "I do feel so funny."

The manager rushed at the sick man. "If you feel funny, go on by all means. It will be the chance of your life," he said wildly.

TEACHER.—"A person was born in the year 1885. What age are they now?"

CLASS (in unison).—"Man or woman?"

MASTER.—"What made that customer walk out without buying anything?"

SHOP-ASSISTANT.—"I'm blowed if I know. He asked for a hat to suit his head and all I did was to show him a soft hat."

JUDGE (to prisoner, aged sixty).—"The sentence is twenty years' penal servitude."

PRISONER (in tears).—"My lord, I shall not live long enough to serve the sentence."

JUDGE (in a kindly tone).—"Never mind, do what you can."

SMART LADY (to plausible beggar).—"And were you really a prisoner for ten years?"

BEGGAR—"Ten years to a day, lidy."

SMART LADY.—But the war did not last ten years."

BEGGAR.—"I ain't talkin' about the war."

"I sent a copy of my new book to the editor of the 'Broadway Review' and he wrote me back such a nice, kind letter?"

"What did he say?"

"Well, he said he would lose no time in reading it."

SHE.—"I see in the papers that they are going to put up a statue to the man who invented rubber tyres."

HE (having had some).—"Wouldn't a bust be more to the point?"

LADY (describing her daughter's engagement).—"Of course, there is rather a big difference between their ages. She is twenty and he is forty-five."

POLITE FRIEND.—"What a pity, because though it doesn't matter now, what about it when she's forty and he is ninety?"

DEAR OLD SOUL (to tramp).—"Here's a shilling and I'll give you a good hint. The lady next door wants her garden dug."

W. WILLIE.—"Much obliged, lidy, for the warnin'."

Newspaper Cutting.—" The strike at the local gas works was declared off and two thousand men were thrown into work."

It was a very slow train and it had kept on stopping. It stopped again and two heads popped out of adjacent carriage windows.

" Come on, chum," said one of the heads, " let's get out and pick some flowers."

" Don't be funny," said the guard, who was pacing up and down the embankment, " there ain't no flowers here."

" Oh, but I've a packet of seed," retorted the head in question.

INDEX

AUTHORS QUOTED